THE *Walkers*
of Southgate and Middlesex
A CRICKETING FRATERNITY

The Walker Brothers founded Southgate Cricket Club in 1855 and Middlesex County Cricket Club in 1864.

Compliments about the brothers, their influence on cricket generally and Middlesex County cricket in particular are legendary.

- I.D. Donnie Walker rendered services to cricket which could not be extolled too highly. *Cricketing Reminisces and Personal Recollections by W.G. Grace.*

- It is difficult to overestimate the services which the Walkers of Southgate rendered to the game of cricket. *The Walkers of Southgate (1900) by W.A. Bettesworth (Sussex 1878-1883).*

- The Walkers created Middlesex County Cricket Club in 1864 and were a family which, in cricketing terms may be ranked with the Graces and the Lyttletons. *The Book of Cricket by Sir Pelham Warner (Middlesex CCC 1894-1920).*

- The Walkers, in short, were Middlesex for a long time. The Walkers of Southgate, most decidedly, stand apart. *Cricket Memories by Edward Rutter (Middlesex CCC 1862-1876).*

- To Mr V.E. Walker we gave, last season, the credit of being the best all round cricketer in the world. We have no reason to alter our opinion, as the figures in the batting and bowling department will justify the statement. *Lillywhites' Guide to Cricket 1860.*

- The Walkers were the mainstay of Middlesex County Cricket Club. *Professor Thomas Case (Middlesex 1864-1868).*

- Southgate, in 1869, had the reputation of being the best ground in England. *Mr C.K. Francis (Middlesex CCC 1870-1879).*

- No names shine out brighter than those of The Walkers of Southgate. *David Buchanan (Warwickshire 1882-1886).*

- The celebrated brotherhood of Southgate. *Barclays World of Cricket by E.W. 'Jim' Swanton.*

- I doubt if any county can boast of a brotherhood of such fine physique and such genuine all round sportsmen as the Walkers of Middlesex fame. *The Jubilee Book of Cricket by Prince Ranjitsinghi (Sussex 1895-1920).*

- That fine ornament and enthusiastic notary of cricket, R.D. Russie Walker. *The Memorial Biography of Dr W.G. Grace by Lord Cobham.*

- Instrumental in the formation of the Club were the Walker brothers of Southgate, who not only played a pivotal role in Middlesex's early off-field administration they also provided some of the most celebrated players in the first two decades of the club's existence. *Middlesex CCC Website (History).*

- No family, with the exception of the Graces, have had so wonderful cricket history as the Walkers of Southgate. *A History of cricket by H.S. Altham (Hampshire 1919-1923).*

- In the 1880's Middlesex CCC depended for its very livelihood upon such benefactors as the veritable host of brothers, the Walkers of Southgate. *Cricket and the Victorians by Keith A. Sandiford.*

- The history of English cricket will be told over and over again, but it can never be related adequately by a chronicler who does not place the Walker Brothers amongst those Lords of the willow, who have in every honourable and brilliant way made the annals. *The History of Cricket by Eric Parker.*

- V.E. Walker was the finest amateur all-rounder of his day. *For the Love of the Game by David Lemmon.*

- The famous Walker family, whose name is indissolubly associated with Middlesex cricket by their instrumentality in establishing the County club. *A Few Short Runs by Lord Harris Kent CCC 1870-1911).*

*To Darb,
with all my love
and thanks for everything*

Introduction and acknowledgements

I have been a member of Southgate Cricket Club for almost 50 years, a Vice President for over 30 and was extremely proud to be President for eight years, but my first tentative visit to The Walker Ground was at the age of seven when the ground was host to the Middlesex CCC beneficiaries of the day. I think that was the start of the love affair!

The story of the Walker Brothers was virtually unknown to me and to most Club members of recent times. The only connection was that in days gone by, not too long ago, at the Annual Club Dinner there were two official toasts. One was to our Queen and the other to the Walkers. As we all raised our glasses invariably there would be a cry from some clever individual who shouted 'and the non-walkers!' This always received the odd guffaw but now, in retrospect, it was rather discourteous to our Club's founders without whom there would have been no cricket club and certainly no Annual Dinners! Their story is an extraordinary one and without doubt will never be repeated. The combination of seven brothers of enormous wealth sharing a great love of the game of cricket is unique.

I must admit to the fact that way back in the year 1900 a book on the same subject was published by a W.A. Bettesworth, a county cricketer at the same time as the brothers and I am indebted to his tome for certain aspects of my book, although I deliberately declined to use too many of the extensive statistics he included.

I am also indebted to Mr Neil Robinson of MCC, Chief Librarian at Lord's, with whom I spent many winter hours in the library, mainly in silence, as I researched every conceivable book which may or may not have had a comment or story about the brothers. At the same time I should posthumously thank the great man of cricket Christopher Martin-Jenkins who had donated to MCC the beautiful rosewood desk at which I mostly sat.

I must also thank Mr Philip Dawson of Christ Church, Southgate, who furnished me with some interesting facts about his church.

I must apologise for the fact that having spent literally thousands and thousands of hours within walking distance of the church, until my recent visit for research reasons I had not actually been inside since I was a six year old pageboy at my sister's wedding.

Mr John Clark of Enfield Council was also very helpful as he provided various pieces of information and photographs pertaining to the brothers.

Sincere thanks to family friend, Jeremy King, from his hacienda in Southern Spain, who helped tremendously with the design and presentation of this book.

Finally, and most important of all, I must thank my wife, Barbara and my three sons for their patience as I continually quoted new snippets about the Walkers at every opportunity. Luckily the three boys are sportsmen and they fully understand these matters. Barbara too, is keen on cricket and football at least, but her patience was tried excessively as I disappeared to my office and my computer to scribe some further item on my chosen subject. I hope you'll agree the story of The Walkers of Southgate and Middlesex is a fascinating subject.

The Walkers of Southgate ... and Middlesex

The Walker family

Arnos Grove

Early cricket at Chapel Field

Middlesex CCC

MCC and the Gentlemen

John Walker

Alfred Walker

Frederic Walker

Arthur Henry Walker

V.E. Teddy Walker

R.D. Russie Walker

I.D. Donnie Walker

Christ Church

The Walker Ground Trust

Southgate CC – The Legacy

The Walkers at Southgate

The Walker Family

This is the remarkable story of the Walker family of Southgate and in particular, the seven cricketing brothers.

The Walkers are the only family in the world known to have provided seven brothers to play for a First class cricket team, a record unlikely to be beaten or even matched.

Isaac Walker, grandson of the original owner of Arnos Grove and his wife Sofia, had twelve children, five daughters, all of whom married, and seven sons who didn't. People said they were married to cricket. Maybe they were but their lives included far more than just cricket.

Some may say that the children were born with the proverbial spoons in their mouths as they all lived together in the grandest and most imposing house for miles around, Arnos Grove, set in over 300 acres of beautiful green pastures.

Others may say that the seven brothers were born with cricket bats replacing the spoons but that would not be quite true as surprisingly, their father had little or no interest in cricket.

Isaac Walker was nonetheless a most imposing figure as he strolled round Southgate village in his silk stockings and knee breeches, as befitting the role of an old-fashioned country squire, which, to all intents and purposes, he was. His brother, Henry, however was a fine cricketer, known especially for his skilful left arm bowling, and he encouraged his nephews to play the game. He was a good enough player to have twice represented the Gentlemen against the Players.

The seven Walker brothers initially learnt their cricket at their respective prep schools, the five eldest in Stanmore and R.D. (Russie) and I.D. (Donnie), the youngest, at Bayford, in Hertfordshire, a private boarding school with only 18 pupils, where they played cricket virtually every day in the summer months.

The three eldest, John, Alfred and Frederic went on to Cambridge University and the younger four, Arthur, V.E. (Teddy), R.D. (Russie) and I.D. (Donnie) all attended prestigious public school, Harrow, with Russie subsequently attending Oxford University.

It's a sobering thought to imagine what the school and university fees must have been!

However, there is little doubt that Isaac could afford the fees as he was a Director of the famous Brewery, Taylor Walker, which was very much a booming and expanding Company in those early days. The Walkers and their near neighbours the Taylors, who lived in nearby Groveland's House, later a hospital, in grounds which subsequently became Groveland's Park, were closely connected in many ways. Originally, both families were Quakers and rather obliquely, united in business in 1816 when Isaac, at the age of 22, became a partner in the Taylor Brewery Company in Limehouse, East London. Seven years later he was to marry Sarah Sofia Taylor and the Taylor Walker union was further cemented.

The original brewery had a rather chequered history of ownership over its first 100 years of existence but the union between Taylor and Walker gave the Company new impetus.

It was, at the time, one of three Quaker owned Brewery giants in London.

By 1868 it was exporting beers to India and Australia as well as supplying pubs throughout the UK and was brewing from an increasingly large site in Limehouse, East London.

Thus the famous Taylor Walker Brewery was founded and it continued trading under the same name until 1959 when it was taken over by Ind Coope. By this time it also owned no less than 1,360 pubs with over 600 in London alone.

Although Taylor Walker has now ceased to exist their famous iconic 'lamps' are still on display today at a number of hostelries around the country as part of a marketing plan by the new owners.

A very successful business and the Walker and Taylor association laid solid foundations for that success.

Emma Loveday Walker, one of the sisters of the cricketing brothers, married a Richard Bradshaw and in time his two sons, John and Robert became Directors of the Company, so the family connection remained strong, even after the passing of the last of the Walkers.

The Taylor and Walker families also combined under the title of 'Separationalists' and operated a private green belt policy in their combined 600 acres by not allowing any building despite the advent of the Great Northern railway bringing many people by train to local stations at Palmers Green and Winchmore Hill. In many ways this did not tie in with the

Walker's famous generosity but in time they relented and Southgate became the thriving suburb that it is today.

In 1851 it was recorded that there were 11 full time servants and a governess living at the house. At that particular time the governess would have been responsible for just the five youngest children aged between 7 and 14. A daunting task but hopefully she had a little assistance from some of the five Walker daughters, who incidentally, though rarely playing cricket themselves were staunch and loyal supporters of their brothers in their chosen sport. Unfortunately, the recent escalation of interest in ladies cricket arrived about 150 years too late for the Walker sisters, but there is no doubt that if it had arrived in their youth, they too would probably have played County cricket as well as their brothers.

As can be seen from the accompanying details the sisters all married and married well, either into the church, into law or into business. With the exception of Anna Maria they each produced large families and to this day most of their descendants include the name Walker in their forenames.

The Walker Sisters

Sarah Sophia: 1824-1902. Married Charles Butler.
Two sons and two daughters.

Anna Maria: 1825-1916. Married the Reverend J. Baird.
No children.

Lydia Louise: 1831-1867. Married Stanhope Ashleigh.
Two sons and three daughters.

Fanny Elizabeth: 1838-1892. Married Fred George.
Two sons and 7 daughters.

Emma Loveday: 1835-1902. Married Captain Richard Bradshaw RN. 5 Sons and 1 daughter.

The brothers devoted their lives to cricket, arranging teams and matches of the highest standard on their own ground and around the country. They travelled to local away games in their own carriage drawn by four handsome horses or by train to more distant venues. They played for various teams all over the country.

The Walkers were enormous donors to over 100 charities and were described as generous patrons of educational, religious and cultural organizations. However, the family, despite their amazing generosity, were mainly secretive about their gifting.

They donated also to the MCC Benefit Fund and The Cricketers Fund Friendly Society for 'cricketers in distress', charities especially close to their hearts.

Another typical piece of their philanthropy was when, in 1884, Teddy promoted and organized a 'charity' match between 'Smokers' and 'Non smokers'. This single match raised the extraordinary amount of £560 for charity, a remarkable sum at the time.

They were all great enthusiasts of this most noble game and encouraged people young and old to play and, if required they would pay all expenses for the matches and indeed, when necessary, those of the players themselves. The brothers were famous for their hospitality before and after matches on their own cricket ground. Most teams were invited to dinner after the match at the big house and many players were invited to stay overnight. The Grace brothers W.G and E.M, when they played at Southgate, and their parents, were amongst many who were grateful recipients of the Walker generosity as they too, were overnight guests at Arnos Grove.

However, the brothers mother, Sofia, did not encourage certain antics and in particular, the habit of smoking. The eldest son, John, thus built an annexe to the main house where they could drink, smoke and socialize to their hearts' content... and it seems they did exactly that! For extra enjoyment a billiards table was provided.

However, more sober activities took place in the main house on Sundays when John played the organ whilst his brothers handed out hymn books for all the guests to join in some community singing. The multi-talented brother R.D. Donnie

Walker was also a fine organist capable of playing several pieces from oratorios.

The brothers knowledge of the game of cricket was unequalled and their captaincy skills were second to none as they were all great students of the game and its idiosyncrasies.

They were gentlemen with all the rather old-fashioned values relating to that particular genre. They were modest, generous, and popular amongst all communities and highly regarded by all who knew them.

In their cricket when they played together it was remarkable how they monopolised games, not in a selfish way, but with their all-round contributions, whether batting, bowling, fielding, wicket-keeping or with their captaincy skills.

Their story is unique.

Arnos Grove

Arnos Grove, the magnificent house in which the Walker family lived.

Isaac Walker, prosperous linen merchant, and his wife Elizabeth, bought the house known as Arnos Grove in 1777 and it remained in the Walker family until 1918 when the lone surviving cricketing brother, R.D. Russell Donnithorne, sold to a Lord Inverforth.

The original Tudor Manor house on the site had been initially owned by local landowners, the Arnolde family, and the estate which was actually 'The Grove (or Copse) of the Arnolde family' was known as 'Arnoldes Grove.'

It was colloquially renamed Arno's Grove by local residents and in time the apostrophe was conveniently dropped.

So Arnos Grove was born.

A London Banker called James Colebrook had acquired the house and land from the Arnoldes in 1719 and quickly replaced the original house with the vast and impressive house as it is today, a Grade II listed building. He sold the estate on to Sir William Mayne (later Lord Newhaven) who, in turn, sold it to Isaac Walker.

Isaac and his wife Sophia had ten children and on the death of his father in 1804, the eldest son, John, inherited the house. Isaac set a Walker family precedent by engaging in much local philanthropy, in his case buying food cheaply and selling it even cheaper to the local poor. Upon his father's death John assumed the management of the house and estate and continued these generosities in many different ways. He opened a charity school on the estate in 1812 and encouraged local children to learn the rudiments of reading, writing and arithmetic.

The Walker Primary School, built in 1953, now with over 400 pupils is an excellent legacy to that early establishment today with Christ Church and The Walker Ground, home of Southgate Cricket Club, as its nearest neighbours.

Considerable changes were made to the house, the Walkers invested in beautiful and numerous paintings, antique furniture and various high quality collections. John had a vast mineral collection, accurate details of which he logged religiously. The collection of paintings which overlooked the ornate staircase was generally regarded as the best in the County of Middlesex outside the Royal Palaces. One of the paintings was a 'Lanscroon' mural depicting 'The Triumph of Julius Caesar'

John was a member of The Royal Society and corresponded with many famous scientists of the 18th and early 19th century.

The majestic building itself consisted of three storeys and constructed from brown brick.

This magnificent house stood in over 300 acres of beautifully green parkland and the family were especially proud of the magnificent cedars and stalwart oaks. Plants and trees were imported from all over the world to add to the splendour of Arnos Grove and its surrounds.

The largest oak, close to the entrance to the south west corner of the ground, remains in splendid magnitude and is proudly represented today by the logo on Southgate Cricket Club's shirt.

On odd occasions in this modern world a cry of 'Come on you Trees' can be clearly heard from the middle as the home captain encourages his team.

That historic old oak has an important and quite unique part to play in the continuing activities and very existence of the Club and the Walker Ground as it is known today.

In 2009, to mark the death of Southgate Cricket Club stalwart, Jim Conroy, a former Club captain and President, a special circular seat was attached to the tree which further enhances its importance to the Walker Grounds' heritage.

Actually Jim, suitably a bachelor, whose enthusiasm and knowledge for the game of cricket was unequalled, would have made the perfect eighth Walker brother with his sociability, his generosity, his cricketing knowledge and his popularity.

He was from Yorkshire and as the Walker family originated from even further north than that they would also have shared a typical Northern determination for winning. The Walkers were great competitors, great tacticians but sporting and chivalrous losers (although losing was not a regular event in their sporting or commercial lives!)

In the first half of the nineteenth century Isaac and John were clearly the popular family names for the eldest sons because Isaac was succeeded by son John in 1804, John's son Isaac took over in 1830, and then upon the death of Isaac, John succeeded in 1852 at the age of 26.

With seven brothers now it became even more complicated and ownership of Arnos Grove was passed from brother to brother with the eldest living brother taking over so that when eldest John died in 1885, it was passed to Frederic; Teddy assumed ownership upon the death of Frederic in 1889 and when Teddy died Russie took over in 1906 until the house was sold in 1918.

When Russie assumed ownership upon the death of his brother he had already been happily living in Regents Park for some time and was not keen to move back to Arnos Grove. So, for a few years the house lay empty.

In 1928 the house was sold to Northwest Electricity (later to become the Eastern Electricity Board) to be used as offices and the Company continued the Walker cricketing tradition by forming its own cricket team, Northmet House, who played for many years at their own beautiful bijou ground in nearby Winchmore Hill.

Naturally, the house was now locally known as Northmet House and remained a very high profile part of the local Southgate community providing many local people with employment. The Company built an extension to the South of the building in 1929 and one to the North in 1935 thereby increasing the size of the building considerably.

After nearly 50 years with the same Company the house was then sold, in 1975, to Legal and General Insurance who immediately changed the name to Southgate House.

They too were encouraged to play cricket and hired the Walker Ground two or three times each year for evening matches until, in 1997, they moved their headquarters to Cockfosters.

Finally, in 1998 the old house became an upmarket residential home for older people and was re-named 'The Beaumont Nursing Home', which it remains.

Today, it remains a most imposing building as it nestles quietly but still majestically behind a bank of trees in Cannon Hill, near the picturesque Southgate Green, and it is still an important and historic local landmark.

Cricket at Chapel Field

A lady in white strolling in the grounds blissfully unaware that a game of cricket was going on in Chapel Fields.

Chapel Field was the designated area within the Arnos Grove estate where cricket was played.

It was initially an area of rough pasture opposite the Weld Chapel (Christ Church) hence the name.

It was indeed a very bumpy wicket and in 1851 eldest brother John arranged for the 'square' to be re-laid to ensure that a higher standard of cricket could be played at the ground and his teenage brothers Teddy and Arthur assisted with the work. He laid out an area on which to play cricket and encouraged not only his own family but also local villagers to play the game.

John formed the original Southgate Cricket Club in 1855.

Some years later he laid out a second adjoining ground specifically for the villagers to play and the brothers took their turn in offering their services as umpires.

The villagers' team was known as Southgate Albert but after a few years the name was changed to Southgate Adelaide and this club, still playing at The Walker Ground to this day is due to celebrate its' 150th anniversary in 2020.

Two nephews of the brothers, John and R.S. Bradshaw, were the first two Presidents of the Adelaide Club.

However, John Walker was not totally satisfied with the early results of the villager's games and decided that they would be helped considerably by the appointment of a professional coach. So, George Hearne, the former Middlesex County professional was engaged.

John Walker's advice to Hearne was 'These villagers can't play cricket. They believe that if they win one in three matches they have done something to be proud of. I want them to play cricket and win at least half of their matches. So, do what you can with them!'.

George Hearne's coaching expertise proved successful as in time the win ratio improved considerably.

George clearly knew what he was doing because he produced three sons all of whom went on to play Test cricket for England.

Over time Walker's Ground became regarded as 'the Mecca of Cricket' and many believed it to be the best ground in the whole of the country. However, only the highest standard of play and conduct was accepted, and although most expenses were covered by the Walkers, invitations were not handed out lightly.

Often matches were advertised in the local press, especially when the All England team were playing and with tents and bunting around the ground and often with Band of the Life Guards playing, there was a true carnival atmosphere. A drummer boy, too, was engaged to entertain the crowds in the intervals. Special trains would be run by the Great Northern Railway to the nearest train station, Colney Hatch (later New Southgate) to bring in extra spectators from all over London and attendances were, at times, substantial.

W.G. Grace was one of many famous cricketers to play at the ground, by now often referred to as Walker's Ground. In 1868 he was invited to play for the United South against John Walker's fifteen. Although he was still only 20 his reputation was such that 10,000 people attended the match and the band of the Life Guards again enlivened the scene.

He top scored in the match with 68 but the match was spoilt somewhat by rain which badly affected the wicket.

No covers in those days!

The team entitled the United South of England was the third and final combination in the triumvirate of teams of professional cricketers who toured the country playing against Clubs and Universities.

The original team was known as the All England XI (AEE) and formed by a William Clarke in 1846.

He was a businessman and cricketer from Nottingham, regarded as something of a 'crusty' character, who recognized the commercial potential of a game which was becoming more and more popular. He also recognized the need to promote his team in other ways and his players were all decked out in white shirts with pink spots.

With the advent of a national railway service he recognized the relative ease with which his players could travel and his teams played at venues all over the country and he made a very decent living out of the scheme. He certainly had no pangs of conscience about the fact that often his team had to travel by train overnight in very uncomfortable conditions.

He was inundated with offers from clubs and others who were prepared to pay him a fee for the benefit of a visit from his travelling 'circus' of professional cricketers, out of which he paid the costs and expenses of his players. Quite apart from his obvious business acumen clearly he was a pretty reasonable cricketer, because, in 1855 for instance, he took no less than 476 wickets in all matches.

However, there was mutiny afoot as, after a few years the players, led by John Wisden (famous cricketer; famous name!) considered that they were being seriously underpaid, as a result of which they left Mr Clarke's organization and formed a new team, entitled similarly, United England X1 (UEE).

The Walker brothers spread their wings quite widely in terms of teams they represented at that time and they each played against these professionals for such diverse teams as:
The Earl of Stamford's XXII; Oxford and Cambridge Combined Universities' XVI; A Luton XXII; Mr E.W. Vyse Esq.'s XXII; XXII of Reigate and XV of MCC.

Between 1858 and 1863 John Walker invited them to play an annual match at his own ground against his own team, John Walker's Southgate XV. Note each of the host teams considered it essential to outnumber the opposition.

This numerical superiority clearly proved successful in Walker's case as they won five out of six games and the 1861 fixture was won by the comfortable margin of 15 wickets!

Work that one out!

In 1858 all seven Walker brothers played for 'John Walker's sixteen against United All England with John captaining the side.

Subsequently, yet another team was formed entitled The United South of England and they came to Southgate between 1866 and 1868.

Many of the great players of the time played for these teams including Wisden, Caffyn, Willsher, Jupp, Alfred Mynn, the Hearnes, the Lillywhites and of course, the Graces.

W.G. actually played three times at the ground over the years and invariably attracted a sizeable crowd.

Actually, W.G. Grace's maiden first class game was actually some time earlier when he represented the Gentlemen of the South against the Players of the South at The Oval. Donnie Walker also made his debut for the Gentlemen of the South that day and what a debut.

In a two innings match 'Donnie' (7 wickets) and W.G. (13 wickets) bowled unchanged throughout the match to bowl the Players out for 79 and 96.

In those days such an event was very unusual because the Gentlemen were regarded as being much stronger in the batting department than in bowling.

An interesting parallel between then and some 150 years later is that both W.G., and in the present day Kevin Peterson, were perceived to have a weakness against left arm spin.

That may or may not be the case but they both seemed to manage their batting well enough despite that apparent deficiency in their play.

One match where G.F. featured heavily, rather than his brother W.G., was a game at Nottingham in 1870 between the Gentlemen of the North and The Gentlemen of the South. By this time of his career people were flocking to see the great man bat but on this occasion he was out relatively quickly. This opened the door, so to speak, for his brother and another famous brother I.D. Walker, to prove to the assembled throng that they, too, had something to offer. In fact, their offering was a stand of 288 with Grace scoring 189 and Donnie 179.

Poor Mr G. Strachan, next man in, waited six hours in the pavilion for his turn to bat and was then out second ball.

That innings of W.G's was a relative failure but a genuine one occurred when playing for the United South of England at Southgate in his second game at The Walker Ground in 1866.

On this occasion he made 0 and 2. This was a rare event indeed because quite apart from his batting failures, unusually, he did not bowl in either innings. Normally the Grace brothers, any two from three, or all three, would bowl between them, an extremely high percentage of the overs.

W.G., of course, although easily the most famous was just one of three cricketing brothers. Brothers E.M. and G.F. too, were excellent players.

On one occasion Donnie Walker and E.M. Grace were playing in a match, rather bizarrely representing Gentlemen of Surrey against United South of England at the Oval.

Bowling in harness, attempting in vain to dismiss one of the day's outstanding batsmen, G.H. Jupp, captain Walker suggested to Grace that he might try bowling very high lobbed full tosses. This he did and at only his second such attempt, the ball, having been lobbed very high indeed, landed precisely on top of the stumps. Upon this there was uproar in the crowd, a number of whom ran on to the pitch in protest whilst Grace picked up a stump in self defence. It was over an hour before play was resumed.

Such anger may have been caused by some sort of betting which was very prevalent at the time. Often there would be large stakes on offer, sometimes up to 1,000 guineas per team, quite apart from individual betting amongst the crowd.

A typical example of the variation and importance of betting at the time was in a match at Southgate between sixteen of the home Club and the United All England XI.

The betting at the start was 6 to 4 on the 'Sixteen' (Southgate) but when the England team were dismissed for just 99 in the first innings it changed to 9 to 1 on the 'sixteen' and 5 to 1 if the 'sixteen' could win by an innings.

In a fluctuating game the home team were set just 78 to win at which point the betting was now 5 to 1 on Southgate to reach their target. In fact, they were bowled out for 55, 23 runs short of their target.

No doubt there were a lot of financial losers and a few winners that day, not least the 'unofficial' bookmakers.

Gambling could be a dangerous drug at that time as indeed, it still is today.

One match at Chapel Field included a most extraordinary bowling performance by Ted Willshire playing for United All England against Walker's XV. Left handed and regarded as one of the best bowlers around at the time, Willsher bowled unchanged to finish with the extraordinary bowling figures of

27 overs, 26 maidens, one wicket, two runs! Only Russie Walker, who somehow eked out two runs, was able to score off him.

This actually asks a lot of questions but unfortunately none of the answers are readily available.

At this time an over consisted of just four balls which helps a little to explain the performance but it was still an incredible statistic. The content of overs was increased to five in 1888 and to six in 1900 and in the UK, at least, has remained that number ever since, although there was a short-lived experiment in 1939 to increase to eight deliveries per over. The idea for eight ball overs caught on in Australia for a while and actually lasted until the seventies.

Another answer to the low scores and indeed slow scoring in general, would be that with between fifteen and twenty two fielders it was rather more difficult to pierce the field, however talented you were, than if the batsmen were faced with just the normal eleven.

Also, of course, the quality of pitches on which to bat would not have received very high marks from today's league umpires in their end of match reports.

Another example of how cricket was rather different in those days is a match in 1874 when Southgate entertained a wandering team entitled 'Will-o-the-Wisps', a club which included some of the best amateur batsmen of the time. It was a one day match and Southgate scored 417-5 with four of the Southgate side and all of the opposition not getting a bat.

End of game!

Russie must have felt a little guilty about that because he became that club's Hon. Secretary from 1877 to 1884.

Southgate were prolific scorers on their own ground during this period with large totals of 494 against Surrey in 1863, 508 against Free Foresters in 1867 and 491 against The Butterflies in 1869.

Unlike the fixture with The Will-o-the-Wisps on each of these occasions the visiting teams were allowed to bat.

A few years later, a Herbert Hewett, playing for Free Foresters, scored 249 against the Club, which remains the highest for a visiting club player.

The organization and planning for matches at The Walker Ground was immaculate in the hands of John Walker, in direct contrast to some of the away fixtures. A fixture between Middlesex and Buckinghamshire at Newport Pagnell is an excellent example of that with a humorous side to it as well.

Both teams and umpires turned up, a fair journey from London in those days with no motorways, to find a rather barren area of common land with little sign of anything remotely resembling a cricket pitch. There were no pitch markings so the umpires asked a local chap, who may or may not have been the actual groundsman, to fetch a length of wood exactly seven foot in length so that they could mark out the necessary. After a while he returned after a visit to the local funeral directors with a coffin lid.

Perfect!

The Walkers encouraged the game locally and often they called on 'a villager' to make up the numbers for their teams. One such was the village barber, Robbins, an eccentric and jovial individual who invariably wore a scarlet jersey and was further conspicuous by a long black beard.

One match which the Walkers organized when all the servants on the estate were invited to play was the annual 'Married' against 'Single' match where not everyone playing quite understood the basic laws of the game.

'Old Billy', the head woodman, batted as if he were chopping down a tree and inevitably made little or no contact with the actual ball. Eventually, he jumped further out of his crease, completely missed the ball and was stumped by some distance.

He was given out by umpire Mr. V.E. Walker.

Despite his belief that Mr Walker was supposed to be a great judge of the game Old Billy was amazed by the decision and queried the ruling to be told that, unfortunately, he was indeed out because he was 'out of his ground'.

His reply, somewhat vexed, was 'How can you be out of your ground in a seventeen acre field?'

A response which has a certain amount of logic to it!

A group of villagers. Maybe a Smokers v Non-Smokers match, a Married v Unmarried or on this occasion maybe Big Bats against Little Bats.

In 1859 the Walkers arranged a match at the ground for the local 'Loyal Adelaide Lodge' to celebrate their 15th anniversary. Teddy and brother Arthur agreed to umpire but clearly interpreted the run out law a little differently to the actual players.

During the match no less than eleven batsmen were run out and one was recorded as having 'walked out'.

On another occasion Teddy and Julius Caesar (not in full Centurion costume!) were playing for the United XI against a country XXII where amongst other amusements a coconut shy had been set up for the entertainment of spectators. The match was petering out to a dull draw with the last pair batting out time when the ball was hit past Caesar who pursued the ball but instead of picking it up he took hold of a loose coconut which he threw with some considerable power to the wicket-keeper. Wicket-keeper Lockyer, one of the best around at the time, whipped off the bails, put the coconut up his jumper and walked off followed by everyone else.

The match was won!

Away from Southgate three of Walkers played a single wicket match against three of Caesars at the latter's home ground in Godalming in Surrey. For no apparent reason the challenge match seemed to last for a long, long time and ended up with the scores equal.

Referring to Caesar incidentally raises an interesting parallel to the present day as, similar to the famous Edrich family of Norfolk, the Caesar family of Godalming could field a cricket eleven consisting entirely of family members.

Tom, grandson of the Middlesex and England batsman Bill, joined Southgate straight from Haberdashers Askes School in 2010, plays regularly for the Club 1st XI as a top order batsman and is currently vice-captain.

Charles Thornton and David Buchanan, a Scot, were two more players who had interesting memories of playing at Chapel Fields.

Buchanan was regarded as one of the best bowlers of the day. In the first 18 years of his cricketing career, mainly in Scotland, he bowled 'fast right hand' but legend has it that he had the misfortune to kill a batsman and was so overcome with remorse he changed his action completely to left arm slow.

He would no doubt have bowled in that style at Southgate when one, Charles Thornton, scored a magnificent 185 for Free Foresters against the Walkers XI.

Thornton, it would seem, was a most unorthodox batsman. A 'slogger' in today's terminology and at that time his batting was described by a fellow player, rather unkindly, as a series of 'blind swipes'.

In this match at Southgate he was dropped by an errant fielder off Buchanan over 100 yards away.

When he was finally dismissed Buchanan stated 'Right, now we can play some proper cricket'.

Another example of how Thornton was regarded by 'proper' cricketers was when, having opened the batting with Donnie Walker in a Walker's XI match at Uppingham School and having reached his 50 at a far faster rate than his partner, he was disappointed when after the game H.H. Stephenson, the Uppingham coach, presented a bat to Walker but not to Thornton. Explaining his decision to Thornton he said 'Mr Walker plays cricket. You don't!'

He played without pads and gloves and was known as 'the hitter of the century'.

He was definitely no purist, but would definitely have attracted a hefty price in today's IPL or Big Bash auctions.

However, Charles Thornton's love of cricket shone brightly enough and in 1871 he invited Donnie and Russie up to Scarborough for a fortnight's cricket, where they each made fine contributions to an event which, in time became known as The Scarborough Festival.

C.I. Thornton, the 'slogger', was regarded as the founder of the famous festival. He bowled daisy cutters in the style immortalised 100 years later by Australian Trevor Chappell.

The Reverend Canon McCormick, a former captain of Cambridge University, was another who played occasionally at the Walker Ground, including once for England against The Walkers when he took 16 wickets in the match. He also played alongside Teddy and Donnie for the Gentlemen against the Players and considered that a catch by Teddy on that occasion, taken a few inches off the ground, was one of the best he had ever seen.

It seems, for some unknown reason there was some prejudice against clergymen taking part in cricket in the days after he was ordained and he sometimes played under an assumed name such as 'J. Cambridge' or 'J. Bingley', the former being his University and the latter his school, Bingley Grammar.

He nonetheless retained his reputation as being one of the best bowlers of his time and played first class cricket, albeit intermittently, from 1854 to 1866.

The Canon was clearly a big shot both in cricket and in the church!

The brothers had played for assorted teams and clubs over the years, home and away, including Clapton, Surrey (rather bizarrely!), Middlesex, MCC, Oxford and Cambridge Universities, the Gentlemen and others previously mentioned. They also hosted numerous games at Chapel Field under the title 'Mr Walkers' team or something similar and, of course, Southgate Albert, the village team for whom the brothers played occasionally, used the ground regularly.

John Walker officially founded Southgate Cricket Club in 1855 and it blossomed, hosting matches against United South of England, Surrey, South Wales, Hertfordshire, and top clubs such as Wimbledon, Richmond and Mitcham from Surrey, Bishops Stortford, Redbourn and Royston from Hertfordshire, and local rivals (still) Enfield and Hornsey.

Also, on the fixture list were wandering clubs all still in existence to this day, Free Foresters, I Zingari, Quidnuncs and Harrow Wanderers.

Not such famous clubs who have since faded from the scene included Tower Hamlets, Harlequins, Islington Albion, The Node, Will-o-the-Wisps CC and The Orientals.

On one occasion a club entitled 'Bruce Castle XVI' from near Tottenham, played against the Club. One wonders whether these were the same group of cricketers who, in 1882, founded Tottenham Hotspur FC, after a meeting under a lamp post in White Hart Lane.

Southgate's early record was excellent and between 1855 and 1877 they suffered only 27 defeats in almost 200 matches.

They were extremely competitive gentlemen, whilst playing the game in the most upright manner.

No charge was made to the public for any major games as most expenses were met by the Walkers.

Playing at Mr Walker's ground, Chapel Field was so popular for the cricket playing fraternity of the day.

Matches there had everything, a beautiful setting, wonderful hospitality and competitive cricket.

All the best players of the time wanted to play there, not only as visitors but also in the colours of the home Club as well.

In that early period of the Club between 1855 and 1877 no fewer than 37 County players represented Southgate CC, some just occasionally but many more regularly.

These included from Middlesex CCC (17), Surrey CCC (8), Kent CCC (6), Sussex CCC (3) and one each from Worcestershire CCC, Warwickshire CCC and Yorkshire CCC.

A true measure of how highly regarded was the venue and the Club and especially, The Walkers.

The brothers were not quite so active at Southgate after 1877 and the day to day running of the club was left to others, although the three youngest brothers played occasionally.

However, John acted as President until his death in 1872. Teddy took over from his brother until he died in 1905 and finally Russie completed the pattern until 1922.

So at least one Walker brother was involved continuously with Southgate Cricket Club as player, administrator or President for over 70 years.

Southgate Cricket Club continued to flourish and was still highly regarded amongst cricket's elite.

Middlesex County Cricket Club

Although there had been a few rather casually organized inter county games for some time the first properly organized County match for Middlesex was against Kent in 1859.

The match, played at Southgate, was arranged and financed by John Walker and resulted in a win for the home side by 78 runs.

The Middlesex team contained notable players of the day such as Wisden and John Lillywhite, four professionals and five of the famed Walker brothers, John, Fred, Alfred, Teddy and Arthur.

In a low scoring game each of the brothers made a contribution of some sort with Teddy quite outstanding with 32 runs in the first innings, the second highest score out of 160, and then a match- winning return of 6-31 in the second innings aided by 2 stumpings by brother John.

The official County Club was formed at a meeting at The London Tavern in Bishopsgate on 2 February 1864. Seventy five enthusiasts attended the meeting and officers were appointed, including a rather unwieldy committee of 16, which included John, Teddy and Donnie, with John Walker and a Mr C. Gordon appointed as Vice Presidents, Mr W. Nicholson as Hon. Treasurer and Mr C. Hillyard as Hon. Secretary.

For that first season John and Teddy were appointed joint captains with Teddy taking full control thereafter. Teddy captained until 1872 at which point brother Donnie succeeded him, continuing in the role until 1884 when for the first time in over 20 years of its existence the position of Club captain was assumed by someone other than a member of the Walker family.

That someone was A.J. Webbe, a fellow Old Harrovian, who had joined the County Club in 1875, captained them for 14 years, later becoming Secretary and finally President until retiring in 1936 after 61 years of service to the Club. Webbe was a very close friend of Donnie Walker and they spent much time together, both on the cricket field and socially, both at home and abroad.

Many years later in 1923, by now President of Middlesex CCC, Mr Webbe was invited to officially open the 'cottage' built at The Walker Ground for the groundsman of the day in memory of his great friend R.D. Walker.

In an emotional speech he spoke eloquently and extremely fondly of the Walker family saying that 'He considered it the greatest compliment to be asked to open the cottage. He was extremely proud of his association with the family, and the way they had showed people the way to play the game and by accepting victory or defeat in similar fashion. His friendship with the family had been the greatest thing in his life and it had been a privilege to know them. The expression 'playing the game' had now been adopted universally but was largely due to the way the Walkers set the example of playing the game in everything in life'.

Heartfelt and sincere words indeed.

Middlesex CCC team of 1884, I.D. Walker, captain, middle of front row.

In 1866 Middlesex CCC won the County Championship for the first time and captain Teddy Walker led from the front, averaging 42 with the bat. Wickets on which people played in those days were somewhat sub-standard so to achieve such a high average at that time was an extraordinary achievement.

During that golden year of 1866 the County also almost beat the touring Australians, losing by one wicket with John Walker scoring 67.

Twelve years later the Club again won the County Championship and this time Donnie was at the helm. Throughout this time, each of the Walkers contributed to the progress of the Club either by playing or administrating at different times but there was always at least one of the brothers and sometimes, all seven, closely involved with the County.

Teddy took over the Presidency of the Club in 1898, succeeding The Earl of Stafford and when he died in 1906 brother Russie took over the reins.

So, when Middlesex won the Championship again in 1920 there had been a Walker family connection with the County throughout the period, 54 years.

The list of captains of Championship winning Middlesex teams makes interesting reading and the two Walker brothers are in illustrious company.

1866	V.E. Walker
1878	I.D. Walker
1903	G. Macgregor
1920	Pelham (later Sir Pelham) Warner
1921	F.T. Mann
1947	R.W.V. Robins
1947	F.G. Mann (shared with Yorkshire)
1977	J.M. Brearley (shared with Kent)
1982	J.M. Brearley
1985	M. Gatting
1990	M. Gatting
1993	M. Gatting
2016	A. Voges

During the early days of the County there were many political and administrative arguments and in 1871 a crisis point was reached. A meeting of members was held to discuss the future of the Club but only thirteen turned up.

Luckily, the assembled group included enough to consider the future was positive and a decision to continue was upheld by just one vote.

Over that period there had been many arguments about which ground to use as the County's home venue. The Walkers and others would have overseen and joined in on many disagreements as the Club moved from Islington Cattle Market to Lillie Bridge, West Brompton and to Prince's in Hans Place, Kensington.

None of these grounds were ideal.

Islington Cattle Market must have presented unusual problems as on Mondays and Thursdays the market sold cattle, sheep and pigs and on Fridays horses, donkeys and goats.

Over 20,000 animals on or near the ground each week!

Perhaps not the ideal conditions to play cricket but nonetheless between 1864 and 1868 the County managed to play no less than 16 games at the venue, which was also triangular in shape. Not an ideal shape for a cricket ground!

The ground at West Brompton was the home of the Amateur Athletic Club and it soon became clear that the place was again totally unsuitable for cricket.

Hans Place, too, hardly lent itself to the specific requirements for the game as the area, very close to the site of Harrods today, was very much a fashionable resort with an adjoining skating rink which attracted a considerable amount of young ladies. The proximity of the rink to the cricket put the ladies in some danger and it was even suggested to the home captain that he should instruct his batsmen not to hit the ball in the direction of the lady skaters.

The situation was so difficult that in 1869 no suitable home ground could be found and the County were forced to play all their matches away from home.

Other venues at Tufnell Park and Alexandra Park were considered but also discarded and by the time of the 1871 meeting, which effectively saved the County Club, only two or three fixtures were being played per season and it took some time before the County was on a reasonable footing again, with six annual fixtures between 1874 and 1878, rising to eight between 1874 and 1880. By the end of the 19th Century County cricket was organized on a much more professional foundation and Middlesex were playing as many as 20 games per season.

A new home had to be found for the County, as all this uncertainty was creating some doubts about its very existence. Some people even wondered whether London could manage a third first class team with Surrey and MCC already in existence.

MCC had made numerous overtures towards the County over the years but Donnie Walker, in particular, was not too keen to move there, partly for financial reasons and partly due to the fiery nature of the Lord's pitches at the time as it was described in those days as 'all ridge and furrow, with at least two shooters per over'. In fact, two counties, Surrey and Sussex, had refused to play there because of the state of the ground.

However, agreement was finally reached and in 1877 the two Clubs agreed terms and have, in general, maintained an excellent working relationship for over 140 years since those early days. Throughout these difficult times the Walkers maintained a constant presence and Teddy, in particular, was a generous benefactor. By 1881 the County was at last on sound financial footing, partly due to Teddy's generosity, but when repayment of the loan was offered to him he was only prepared to accept 50% of the outstanding amount.

This was so typical of The Walker brothers well documented benevolence towards cricket and cricketers, in particular.

The full Middlesex County side did not return to The Walker Ground until 1991 after a break of 132 years, when they entertained Kent in a Sunday League match, coincidentally the same opposition as in 1859.

The County then used the ground regularly over the next few years and between 1998 and 2011 the County played no less than 20 games in various denominations.

It proved to be a happy hunting ground for the home County as their win ratio was extremely high at The Walker Ground.

The first four day County match was against Essex and was notable for a fine innings of 241 by Mike Gatting, in his last season of County cricket. This remains the highest individual score on the ground by a home batsman.

Unfortunately, an administrative and financial disagreement between the County and The Walker Trust soured the relationship and the Walker Ground was thus omitted from the County's list of out-grounds.

Alternative venues were found at Radlett, Richmond and Merchant Taylors School, two of which, ironically, are out of the county.

In recent times much work has been done by representatives of both camps to re-instate the relationship and there is much hope on both sides that it will blossom again soon.

In 2018 there will be two four day County second eleven games at the ground and it is hoped that the following year will see the return of genuine County Cricket.

The contribution of The Walker brothers to Middlesex County cricket was considerable:

- John was a founder member of the County in 1864 and was immediately appointed a Vice-President and their first joint captain with his brother Teddy. He remained a Vice-President until his death in 1885.

- Teddy was also a founder member of the County, the Club's first Hon. Secretary and captain or joint captain from 1864 until 1872. He was President from 1898 until his death in 1906.

- Donnie took over the captaincy from Teddy and continued in the role for 12 years. He was a committee member until his death in 1898.

- Russie succeeded his brother Teddy as President, a position he held until his death in 1922. He too was a committee member throughout that time.

- The other three brothers, Alfred, Fred and Arthur all played for the County at various times between 1850 and 1863. There was an unbroken connection between the Walker fraternity and Middlesex CCC from 1850, when John played his first game for the County against Surrey at Lord's, until 1922 when the last remaining brother, Russie, passed away.

72 years of service from the same group of brothers

An amazing record.

Marylebone Cricket Club and The Gentlemen

Between 1847, when John made his debut and 1884 when Donnie played his last game for the country's most famous Club, the brothers, with the exception of Alfred, played regularly for MCC, with over half of the games being played at Lord's. Altogether, they played over 100 matches for MCC and John, Fred, Donnie and Russie all scored at least one fifty with Russie also scoring a hundred. Teddy did not score big runs but always contributed either with his clever bowling variations, his captaincy or his brilliance in the field.

At that time MCC was still, more or less, a private gentleman's club but there was a certain standard of play and performance required to be selected. There is no doubt each of the brothers proved his worth. Gentlemen are still welcomed into the Club but today there is a 20 year waiting list!

Ladies too, have now been welcomed as players and members in these enlightened times as the ladies game thrives.

MCC was actually founded in 1787 and by the time the Walkers were playing the Club played between 40 and 50 games per year. This rose to about 150 during the 1890's but today MCC plays as many as 500 each year against Schools, Universities, Clubs and touring sides.

They also organize numerous tours all over the world, although England teams playing abroad no longer play under the MCC banner.

Teddy was an MCC committee member and a Trustee of the Club for many years and helped to select MCC teams to represent England overseas in Australia, Canada and the USA.

He was appointed President of MCC which is a measure of his reputation as a talented, knowledgeable and popular member of the cricketing fraternity. Ten years later, sometime after he had retired from cricket, he and brother 'Donnie' were invited by MCC to play alongside W.G. Grace in the Club's centenary match at Lord's for 'The Veterans' against the Gentlemen of MCC. It was not surprising that he was asked to captain the side which he did with his usual style and good humour and slotted comfortably into his favourite fielding position, cover point, as if he had never been away.

The MCC centenary match at Lord's. Donnie Walker on the extreme left and Teddy Walker, third from right, next to W.G. Grace, all in the middle row.

ONE PENNY.

Lord's MCC Ground.

GENTLEMEN OF M.C.C. v. EIGHTEEN VETERANS OVER FORTY.

THURSDAY and FRIDAY, JUNE 16, 17, 1887.

THE VETERANS.

	First Innings.		Second Innings.	
1 C. R. Green, Esq.	c J. Walker, b Webbe	22		
2 I. D. Walker, Esq.	b Grace	6	b Paravicini	51
3 M. Turner, Esq.	b Webbe	16	c R. Thornton, b Robertson	5
4 Rev. C. G. Lane	b Robertson	13	c Grace, b Robertson	18
5 E. Hame, Esq.	b Webbe	23	b Robertson	6
6 Rev. S. C. Voules	c R. Thornton, b Grace	29	not out	20
7 J. F. Leese, Esq.	c Walker, b Robertson	62		
8 J. Round Esq., M.P.	c Leatham, b Robertson	5		
9 Major A. S. Griffiths	b Robertson	4		
10 A. Appleby, Esq.	b Paravicini	19		
11 Major A. W. Anstruther	b Grace	40	b Walker	20
12 C. Booth, Esq.	b Robertson	0		
13 E. B. Rowley, Esq.	c Leatham, b Robertson	2		
14 Colonel N. W. Wallace	c Leatham, b Grace	1	not out	33
15 P. Hilton, Esq.	c Studd, b Robertson	1		
16 Colonel J. Fellowes	run out	15		
17 E. Rutter, Esq.	hit w, b Grace	0		
18 V. E. Walker, Esq.	not out	6		
	B 16, l-b 17, w 3, n-b 1	37	B 18, l-b 6, w , n-b ,	24
	Total	**306**	**Total**	**175**

1-18 2-30 3-51 4-91 5-119 6-143 7-168 8-172 9-209 10-250
1-57 2-36 3-94 4-117 5-121 6- 7- 8- 9- 10-
11-250 12-253 13-259 14-255 15-251 16-293 17-306
11- 12- 13- 14- 15- 16- 17-

GENTLEMEN OF M.C.C.

	First Innings.		Second Innings.	
1 C. I. Thornton, Esq.	b Appleby	22		
2 E. J. C. Studd, Esq.	c V. E. Walker, b Appleby	22		
3 Rev. R. T. Thornton	c and b I. D. Walker	11		
4 T. C. O'Brien, Esq.	st Round, b I. D. Walker	40		
5 J. S. Russel, Esq.	b Fellowes	17		
6 W. G. Grace, Esq.	b Rutter	24		
7 A. J. Webbe, Esq.	b Appleby	104		
8 J. G. Walker, Esq.	c Leese, b Rutter	2		
9 P. J. de Paravicini, Esq.	c Voules, b Appleby	32		
10 J. Robertson Esq.	c Fellowes, b Appleby	0		
11 G. A. B. Leatham, Esq.	not out	1		
	B , l-b 3, w , n-b ,	3	B , l-b , w , n-b ,	
	Total	**278**		

1-43 2-44 3-62 4-95 5-102 6-162 7-207 8-273 9-277 10-278
1- 2- 3- 4- 5- 6- 7- 8- 9- 10-

Umpires—Farrands and Price   Scorers—Clayton and Flanagan.

This is the scorecard of the celebration match with so many famous players of the era.

A good example of the social standing of the Walker family and Teddy Walker in particular is a list of MCC Presidents who preceded or succeeded him in the years leading up to and immediately after his appointment. In fact, after his Presidential year, over the next 40 years, until the beginning of World War II there were only three 'commoners' appointed to the post of President of MCC.

After the war, this ritual slowly changed and in more recent times ex- England Test cricketers have tended to assume the role, although there was at least one alternative when in 1957 Southgate's own, Sir Cyril Hawker, became President.

The second MCC President with Southgate Cricket Club connections in 66 years.

Bally's 'Magazine of Sports and Pastimes', an important periodical of the time, published between 1860 and 1922, wrote ' Regarding Mr V.E. Walker's elevation to President of MCC we are all glad to note the gracefulness and justness which has placed the veteran there '

List of MCC Presidents 1880 to 1897

1880	Sir W. Hart Dyke, Bart, M.P.
1881	Lord George Hamilton
1882	Lord Belper
1883	Hon. R. Grimston
1884	Earl Winterton
1885	Lord Wenlock
1886	Lord Lyttleton
1887	Hon. E. Chandos Leigh, Q.C.
1888	Duke of Buccleuch
1889	Sir Henry James Q.C.
1890	Lord W. Erersby
1891	V.E. Walker Esq.
1892	W.E. Denison Esq.
1893	Earl of Dartmouth
1894	Earl of Jersey
1895	Lord Harris
1896	Earl of Pembroke
1897	Earl of Lichfield

Gentlemen v Players

Whilst on the subject of gentlemen this brings us quite naturally to the annual match between The Gentlemen (amateurs) and The Players (professionals), a match which took place annually, nearly always at Lord's. The series started in 1819 and amazingly continued until as late as 1963, a time when much of this type of elitism had disappeared.

However, in those early days, the class system was rampant and the teams were defined thus: 'The Gentlemen would be members of the middle and upper classes and have been privately educated and The Players would be deemed working class'.

Another similar example of this class distinction was a match at Cambridge University when John and Alfred represented a team entitled 'Those that had been educated at Public Schools' to play against a team who played under the title of 'Those who had not been educated at Public Schools. 'Townspeople' against 'Villagers' was another socially divisive fixture.

It is difficult to believe in today's more open society that such matches could be played but they were a very important part of the social and cricketing fabric of the time and thoroughly enjoyed by all the participants and watched by large crowds.

None of those poor unfortunates who had to be paid to play cricket (The Players) or the 'those who didn't go to Public School' team seemed to mind much either, it seems.

Having said that, it was often felt that some of the amateurs actually earned more from cricket than the professionals and W.G. Grace was at the forefront of those rumours.

The Walker brothers were, of course, excellent examples of the word 'gentlemen ' in every respect and with the exception of Alfred, represented the Gents regularly between 1852 when eldest brother John first played, until 1884 when Donnie played for the last time.

Teddy played in the annual match no less than 25 times and Donnie on 22 occasions and like John, they often captained the team as well. Teddy made his debut for the Gents against the Players at the tender age of 19.

It was generally accepted that in cricketing terms the match was between the classical batting of the amateurs against the aggressive and sometimes earthy bowling of the professionals. For most of the period in which the Walkers played the results certainly didn't favour the blue bloods as between 1851 and 1864, for instance, the Gents won just once, drew another and lost the other 17. The belief was that real amateurs sometime needed to earn a proper living and as they got older they had to retire from serious cricket and the team of amateurs subsequently became somewhat depleted.

The advent of W.G. (playing as an 'amateur') changed the pattern of the matches and while he was playing, between 1865 and 1906, the win ratio went up to 75% for the Gents, yet another example of the extraordinary effect W.G. had on the world of cricket.

However, one of the first victories for the Gents during this period was in 1868 when thanks to a brilliant innings of 165 by Donnie Walker the Players were defeated by an innings. Needless to say, although W.G. failed with the bat on that occasion he starred with the ball.

Teddy was normally captain when he played and took a total of 62 wickets for the Gents in his 25 games. A side issue was of course, the fact that until 1963 when MCC announced that all cricketers should be regarded as professionals the amateurs changed in nice, roomy and comfortable dressing rooms and the professionals in rather more cramped little spaces. The concept of a Gents v Players cricket match, with all its connotations, was definitely from another era.

1852

PLAYED AT LORD'S, JULY 19, 20, AND 21
Result: The Players won by five wickets

The Gentlemen's second innings was notable for a fine innings of 58 by J. Walker, the eldest of the famous Walker family, of Southgate, who founded the club there, and who were so prominent in Middlesex cricket and in the councils of the M.C.C. When the Players went in to score 90 Yonge bowled ten consecutive maidens, but George Parr, with 46, not out, settled the issue.

Alfred Mynn and N. Felix made their last appearances for the Gentlemen. Mynn lives in cricket history, and in these matches he scored 605 runs and took 107 wickets. Felix, who was the first cricketer to wear a cap, if not so prominent, scored 402 runs.

THE GENTLEMEN

First Innings		Second Innings	
W. Nicholson, b. Dean	31	b. Grundy	28
E. Napper, b. Grundy	11	c. Caffyn, b. Martingell	2
A. Haygarth, b. Dean	9	st. Box, b. Martingell	14
H. Vernon, b. Martingell	1	b. Grundy	30
Hon. S. Ponsonby, b. Grundy	32	b. Wisden	0
N. Felix, c. Chatterton, b. Clarke	15	c. Dean, b. Grundy	1
A. Mynn, b. Clarke	15	c. Chatterton, b. Clarke	3
J. Walker, b. Grundy	0	c. Martingell, b. Dean	58
G. Yonge, b. Grundy	1	not out	22
E. Balfour, not out	1	b. Wisden	12
Sir F. Bathurst, b. Grundy	2	b. Martingell	
Leg byes 3, wide 1	4	Byes 7, leg byes 5, wide 1	13
Total	122	Total	187

THE PLAYERS

J. Dean, c. Yonge, b. Bathurst	11	c. Nicholson, b. Yonge	12
J. Wisden, c. Bathurst, b. Yonge	6	run out	2
J. Guy, c. Bathurst, b. Yonge	36	b. Yonge	8
G. Parr, b. Yonge	3	not out	46
W. Caffyn, c. Nicholson, b. Walker	13	c. Felix, b. Mynn	9
T. Box, c. Ponsonby, b. Walker	39	c. Ponsonby, b. Walker	6
W. Martingell, c. Haygarth, b. Yonge	20	not out	3
J. Grundy, not out	69		
G. Chatterton, c. Ponsonby, b. Bathurst	2		
T. Nixon, c. Nicholson, b. Bathurst	0		
W. Clarke, c. Nicholson, b. Bathurst	3		
Byes 12, leg byes 4, wides 2	18	Byes 4, leg byes 2, wide 1	7
Total	220	Total (5 wkts.)	90

An example of a Gents v Players scorecard with John Walker making an important contribution.

John Walker

Born: Palmers Green 1826

Died: Arnos Grove, 1885 aged 59

First Class Career

Cambridge University (1846-1849)

MCC (1847-1863)

A Middlesex XI (1850-1863)

Middlesex CCC (1864-1866)

87 matches

1,355 runs

Highest score 98

Wickets 18

As the eldest brother John truly led the way regarding cricket and although he was regarded as quite easy going he was very much master in his own house. His brothers all regarded him as their head and he was the elder statesman of the family. It was said that when you played against John Walker and his team you had to prepare yourself for a fight to the finish. It is a continuing theme that although the brothers were generous, courteous and well-bred gentlemen they were nonetheless fierce competitors and not at all keen on losing.

John was described as firm but fair and was never slow in giving praise to others.

He spent large sums of money on the ground and arranged matches of all kinds, at home and away and sent many personal invitations for young players to play for his teams. He was insistent that only players of a high fielding standard would be invited.

Although 6ft 2inches tall John was a wicket keeper and had three years in the Cambridge University team in that role, captaining the side in his final year.

In the 1858 fixture with Wimbledon he did not give away one bye in either innings, a very unusual feat in those days.

Possibly his finest innings was the 98 he scored for the Gentlemen against the Players at The Oval in 1862, which subsequently turned out be his highest first class score. In fact, he played 8 times in Gents v Players matches and also captained the side.

He also scored 67 against the visiting Australian tourists in 1886.

He and his brothers were quite innovative in their approach to captaincy and field placings, often moving a fielder's position in response to the batting style of a particular player, very much the norm in the modern game but very unusual in those days.

On one such occasion he hatched a plot with brother Teddy to snare a certain John Wisden. Wisden, described as a 'funny little mite of a man', liked to play the 'Draw' shot, a popular shot of the day whereby a batsman would deliberately hit the ball between his legs and direct the ball in the direction of fine leg. This was regarded as a very skilful art but as time moved on it became regarded with some disdain and with rather less acclaim and in time it became known with a certain amount of derision as a 'Chinese cut', or even the 'Harrow Drive'.

(In recent times, the 'nutmeg' an expression copied from football, describes the shot, and in the 2017 Ladies World Cup, Nat Sciver perfected the shot and it was re-named a 'Natmeg!')

On this occasion the plan was that Teddy would bowl to that strength and wicket-keeper John would step sharply to one side to take the catch.

The plan worked perfectly except for one important aspect.

Teddy's aim was good; John took up the perfect position but, sadly as Wisden successfully played his favourite shot straight to the wicket-keeper, but unfortunately John dropped the catch.

However, it certainly had a psychological effect on Wisden as he declined to play his favourite shot for the rest of the innings. Nonetheless, although not a successful ploy on this occasion it was a classic example of how John thought about the game and its tactics.

Wisden, incidentally, also attended Harrow School and was known as a fast round arm bowler, and regarded as one of the quickest bowlers of his day and a fifteen year County career with Sussex, Kent and finally Middlesex saw him complete his career with a bowling average of 10.12.

On one occasion he took ten wickets in an innings... all clean bowled.

He was also something of an entrepreneur, opening a 'Cricket and Cigar' Business in Leicester Square, owning a pub in Sussex and of course, in 1864 creating the famous Wisden Cricketing Almanac which has become the 'bible' for cricket lovers around the world.

John Walker was a tireless worker for Middlesex County Cricket Club as described elsewhere and was on the MCC committee and for a while, rather bizarrely on the Surrey CCC committee as well.

(In those early days many players changed Counties almost overnight as and when they were invited and it was many years before stricter registrations were introduced).

He was a Vice President of Middlesex CCC from 1864 until his death in 1885, founded Clapton CC with a Mr W. Nicholson for whom he often played, and of course, founded Southgate Cricket Club in 1855.

He started working for the Taylor Walker Brewery at the age of 26 and continued working as a Director of the Company until his death.

As befitted a 'gentleman' of the day he had a great interest in shooting and often, on the day after a match at Southgate he would host a shooting party in the grounds of Arnos Grove. In 1881 John was appointed Chairman of the Southgate Local Board of Health which was the forerunner to the Urban District Council, a measure of his high standing in the local community.

He died in 1885 and the ownership of Arnos Grove passed to the oldest living brother, Frederic.

His funeral was attended by so many past and present cricketers, from 'the highest to the lowest' and Christ Church, opposite the ground, was full to overflowing.

The whole village mourned.

Alfred Walker

Born: Arnos Grove 1827

Died: Arnos Grove, 1870 aged 43

First Class Career

Cambridge University (1846-1848)

A Middlesex XI (1851-1859)

14 matches

95 runs

Highest score 20

Wickets 36

Alfred Walker was over 6ft tall and weighed 14 stone and this power and strength enabled him to become an exceptionally fast right arm under arm bowler. He, apparently, had a great deal of curl from leg but he did not play much first class cricket.

He had a strange approach to the wicket as he took a longish run in a slanting direction from the leg side. Middlesex members may remember John Price the England fast bowler of the sixties as having a similar, angled approach to the wicket, but his was from the off side.

Just before reaching the wicket Alfred would swing his bowling arm sharply behind his back. Umpires were in as much danger as the batsmen and they tended to stand a few yards back from the stumps to avoid contact although one unfortunate gentleman did receive a heavy blow to the stomach from the flailing arm and decided to give himself a couple of yards.

He certainly had some success with his bowling and unusually managed to achieve two separate hat-tricks whilst playing for Southgate Albert in 1853. A feat few bowlers achieve once in their lifetime let alone twice.

Also, in 1850, playing for Clapton in a match against Surrey he took fifteen wickets in the match and with 42 runs he was the game's top individual scorer.

However, Alfred Walker was probably the least successful of the brothers in his cricketing ability but could arguably be described as the most entertaining batsman of them all as he apparently had no interest whatsoever in playing any sort of defensive stroke.

He was the only brother who did not play for the full County team but did represent the team known as 'A Middlesex XI' on a number of occasions.

He was also the only one of the brothers not to represent the Gentlemen against the Players.

Nonetheless, he was obviously a fine cricketer but succumbed to various gout related ailments which curtailed his career.

Like younger brother Russie he created his own fashion style as he often played wearing the brightest scarlet trousers.

He was of generous nature and very popular. A group of players had a collection to aid a fellow cricketer, Fred Lillywhite, who was very ill and fallen on hard times. Alfred, hearing of the collection told the group to return the collection to the individuals and he would, personally, ensure Mr Lillywhite was looked after for the rest of his life.

This he did.

He often spent his winters in Tor Cross in Dartmouth in Devon where he was heavily involved with local boating organizations.

Sadly, he died very young at the age of just 43.

Frederic Walker ('Fred')

Born: Arnos Grove 1829

Died: Arnos Grove, 1889 aged 60

First Class Career

Cambridge University (1849-1852)

MCC (1853-1856)

A Middlesex XI 1859

34 matches

726 runs

Highest score of 71

Wickets 13

He was the shortest of the brothers, standing at 5ft 7 inches, and was a wicket-keeper and batsman. Like so many shorter players before and since, his best shots were the pull and in particular, the cut.

Like all of his brothers except Donnie, Fred suffered badly from rheumatic gout and during one year he took to his bed for months with a particularly bad attack of the malaise.

Clearly, this illness was a great disadvantage to him because he was regarded as one of the best batsmen of his time, exampled by a magnificent innings of 170 in 1857 playing for Walker's team against the might of Surrey Club and Ground at Southgate and as the statistics above suggest he was unable to play quite as often as he would have liked. That excellent innings was the first century for Southgate by a member of the family.

In the inaugural year of Southgate Cricket Club, 1855, he was the first member of the family to score 50.

The following year he was ever-present and played all 14 games for the Club.

He rarely bowled but on one occasion in 1853, playing for Cambridge University against MCC he took six wickets, ably assisted with four stumpings by his wicket-keeping replacement.

His unfortunate health problems were undoubtedly why he did not play more cricket.

In fact, all 7 brothers only played together in the same team twice, once in 1860 and again in 1861. The first match was for John Walker's XVI against United All England, when Donnie, still at Harrow, played aged 16, in a three day match.

The second in the following year was against local rivals, Enfield.

Fred did however, represent MCC on a number of occasions and played three times for the Gents against the Players, twice at Lord's and once at The Oval, where he was joined by three of his brothers, John, Arthur and Teddy.

Sadly, it was hardly surprising he retired early from active cricket and retired virtually an invalid, to a charming cottage in Oxford where he spent many happy hours tending to the many rare and valuable plants in his garden.

Arthur Henry Walker

Born: Arnos Grove 1833

Died: Arnos Grove, 1878 aged 45

First Class Career
MCC (1855-1861)

A Middlesex XI (1859-1862)

23 matches

601 runs

Highest score 90

14 Wickets

As a boy Arthur was a more than useful wicketkeeper with a rather ungainly style.

After he left Harrow he became a round-arm bowler. He was a right handed batsman and was regarded as a big hitter of a cricket ball. Despite his all round ability he always enjoyed reverting back to his role as a wicket-keeper and in 1868, at the age of 35, he managed 6 stumpings, some off his brothers, in a Southgate match against Free Foresters.

Arguably his best performance was for a Gentlemen of England team against the Gentlemen of Kent in 1857 when he scored 90 runs and took a total of 8 wickets in the two innings match.

1857 proved to be his most successful season and he scored more runs for Southgate that year than any of his brothers.

In 1860 he broke a kneecap at the beginning of the season and was unable to play much until September when he was allowed a substitute to field for him and a runner to run for him.

Then again, two years later he broke his thigh playing rugby and this virtually finished his cricketing career but he did play the occasional game for the Club, for whom he was a mainstay during his short life. Sadly, like his elder brother Fred he was unable to have a long first class career due to illness and persistent injuries. A very unlucky sportsman, who sadly died young.

Vyell Edward Walker ('Teddy')

Born: Arnos Grove 1837

Died: Arnos Grove, 1906 aged 69

First Class Career

MCC (1856-1874)

Middlesex CCC (1864-1872)

145 matches

Runs 3,384

Highest score 108

334 wickets

Vyell, or Teddy as he was universally known, was in the Harrow eleven from the age of 15 when he played at Lord's for the first of many times.

He was also outstanding at football, held the racket at Harrow (meaning he was school champion) and was an excellent shot.

He was originally a 'round arm' bowler but lost his action, changed to fast underhand and eventually became a lob bowler. He apparently ran down the wicket after every ball and he is quoted as saying that it helped him gain quite a few wickets. If a batsman was in defensive mode he would run down the wicket so quickly that he was able to catch the ball from a dead-batted prod. On one occasion he was able to lure the batsman into top edging the ball behind the wicket and he ran swiftly, dived and caught a brilliant catch.
He varied his lob bowling cleverly with subtle variations of pace and angle and he mostly bowled round the wicket.

He was unsurpassed as an even-tempered and astute captain and made subtle changes to the field, ideas learned from his elder brother, John. Strangely, he was the first captain to consider the fielding position of extra cover as an option. As a captain he was described as being imperturbable, remaining calm at all times and he 'never worried a man' for a misfield.

At Harrow Teddy was encouraged to bowl lobs by two coaches at the school, the Honourable Robert Grimston and Lord Bessborough.

Of course, not everyone truly appreciated the art of 'lob' bowling.

In a North v South match a gentleman known as 'Ducky' Diver, (the derivation of his name beggars belief!) lost his wicket to a high lob from Teddy and in a fit of temper angrily mowed down his stumps and stormed off the ground.

After the game he was rather embarrassed and subsequently apologised to Teddy for his fit of pique, an apology Teddy accepted with his usual grace.

Underarm, and thus lob bowling slowly lost its attraction as it was clear that there was greater chance of success by bowling over arm, but a few people continued the art for a number of years. The last person to be selected specifically as an underarm bowler was Trevor Moloney who played three games for Surrey as late as 1921 but he had very little success.

Actual underarm bowling remains legal to this day as long as the bowler has the umpire's approval and the batsman has been warned.

Unsurprisingly, at his pace, Teddy rarely required the use of a 'long stop' to his bowling and invariably managed without one but nonetheless at the time it was a popular and important position as the ball scurried along off divots, ridges and furrows and left many a wicket-keeper bemused.

Sadly, for many club wicket-keepers this specialist position has totally disappeared from the game now but there are many who would welcome its return.

There was splendid advice about the position in Nyren's 'Cricketing Guide' published in 1844 when the following useful aid to a wicket-keeper's life was recorded:

'THE LONG STOP holds a most important station in the game of cricket. His appointment is behind the wicketkeeper, and he should stand in, so as to save the one run. When the ball does not come to his hand with a fair bound, he must go down upon his right knee with his hands before him; then in case these should miss it, his body will form a bulwark and arrest its further progress. In addition to this duty he is required to cover many slips from the bat, both to the leg and to the off side. It is a requisite that he should learn to throw with a quick action to the top of the wicket.'

In 1859 Teddy achieved an extraordinary all-round record in consecutive matches as follows:

England v Surrey at the Oval
20 not out; 108 and 14-91
Middlesex v Kent at Canterbury
71 and 8-89
J.Walker's XI v U.E.XI at Southgate
88 and 9-128
Gentlemen of the South v Gentlemen of the North at Liverpool
7 and 69 and 9-161
England XI v Gentlemen of Sussex at Southgate
2 and 69 not out and 10-140

What a tremendous all-round effort by a fine cricketer.

As a bowler he took ten wickets in an innings three times, on the first occasion, in 1859, whilst representing England against Surrey at The Oval. With nine wickets to his name already, he induced a catch from the interestingly named Julius Caesar but sadly the catch was dropped by an erring outfielder. The batsman crossed and very next ball he snaffled the prized wicket of 'Granny' Martingell, an Old Etonian whose batting credentials had little substance, but he nonetheless went down in history as the final wicket in a famous ten wicket haul.

The other occasions when Teddy took all ten wickets were in June 1864 playing for Middlesex against the Gents of Kent and in July the following year playing for Middlesex against Lancashire in Manchester.

Then, there was the one that got away!

Playing for Middlesex against Surrey at the Islington Cattle Market in 1864 Teddy took the first 9 wickets for 62. The final wicket appeared to be stumped as the ball rebounded off the wicketkeeper's pads on to the stumps with the batsman out of his ground. However, the batsman, a Charles Payne, clearly a stickler for the rules, pointed out that he had touched the ball on its way through so that he was actually run out, not stumped.

Despite his success as a bowler, he was also highly regarded as a batsman. He first played for the Gentlemen against the Players aged 19 in 1856 and three years later he scored 108 playing for England against Surrey (the same match in which he took all ten wickets—not a bad return).

He believed that to be his best ever innings but an innings of just 40 on a difficult wicket at the Oval ten years later ran it close, he said.

In 1859 Lillywhite's Guide to Cricketers (The Cricketer Magazine of its day) stated categorically that Teddy was the 'best player in the world' and one year later the same publication gave him a similar accolade for the second year running.

Amongst all this success there was one occasion when Teddy was not quite so successful.

In 1882, Teddy, brother Donnie and Lord Harris were part of a four man selection committee, with a Mr Burbidge, who chose the England team to play Australia in an unofficial Test Match at The Oval. This turned out to be the famous 'Demon' Spofforth's match with the Australian fast bowler taking 14-90 in the match and with England losing by 7 runs.

The following day the team was savaged by the Press and this famous phrase was coined by The Sporting Times:

'In affectionate remembrance of English cricket which died at the Oval on 29 August 1882. Deeply lamented by a large circle of friends and acquaintances. R.I.P.

The body will be cremated and the ashes taken to Australia'.

That, of course was the start of the fiercest rivalry in cricket as England were encouraged to visit Australia as soon as possible to recover 'The Ashes'.

In fact, Donnie retained his position as a selector, along with Lord Harris and the honourable Alfred Lyttleton and a strong team was chosen to do just that in the following winter.

The captain, the honourable Ivo Bligh was given the team and told specifically 'To bring back the Ashes!'

This he did, winning the 'Ashes series' 2-1, but losing a fourth game which had been added to the itinerary but didn't count in the official series.

The Hon. Ivo and his team were successful but must have been very homesick as they were out of the UK for no less than 230 days.

Teddy's judgement of cricket and cricketers was highly regarded and he was often asked his opinion when teams needed special selection and amongst others he selected representative teams to travel to Canada in 1869, USA and numerous others.

He was a magnificent fielder and was highly regarded at cover point. It was said that 'His strength of arm and wrist were apparently so great that he could return the ball to the wicket-keeper like lightning, without any apparent withdrawal of the arm, to the undoing of many a batsman.'

He set very high fielding standards.

Baileys Magazine described his fielding thus: 'He was the grandest fieldsman who ever flannelled'.

He was a great advocate of no boundary lines and once ran an eight and on another occasion ran two consecutive sevens. It is noted that during his time neither Lord's nor the Oval had boundary lines and even hits to the pavilion had to be 'run out', as it was called then.

The record for the most number of runs actually run from one hit was nine. That was in 1842 when the Honourable Frederick Ponsonby managed the feat on Parker's Piece (not surprisingly, a large area of ground in Cambridge) playing for MCC against Cambridge University. The honourable gentleman was no doubt out of breath by the end of the run!

In later life, Teddy, reflecting on his career compared to that of his great rival and contemporary W.G. Grace, stated that the introduction of boundary lines quite early in W.G's. career helped him considerably inasmuch as his weight would not have enabled him to run such distances during an innings.

W.G. was able to hit fours and sixes instead.

Teddy was regarded as the best all-round cricketer of his time until the mighty W.G. appeared on the scene but for a couple of years they were on a par. When batting averages were normally in the twenties in 1866 both Teddy and Grace averaged 42, a measure of how good Teddy actually was.

He was an even tempered, diplomatic and tactically aware captain and was loved by all.

On one occasion, captaining England against Surrey at The Oval in 1868 he kindly gave W.G. Grace leave of absence on the second day of the match to run in a quarter mile hurdles race at the National Olympian Association Meeting at Crystal Palace.

Of course, W.G. won the race in an excellent time of 1 minute 10 seconds, having scored a century the previous day.

Twice, in 1868 and 1872, Teddy was selected in teams to go abroad to the USA, the second time as captain, but on both occasions he had to withdraw for business reasons.

W.G. Grace assumed the role of captain.

Teddy was also captain of England against Surrey at The Oval in 1862 when umpire John Lillywhite no balled one Edgar Willsher six times in succession for 'having his arm too high '. Willsher and the other professionals all walked off the ground in protest whilst amateurs including Teddy, Lord Cobham and the Hon. C.G. Lyttleton remained on the field in support of the umpire. Play did not resume until the following day with a replacement umpire but it did eventually bring about a reform in the law regarding over arm bowling and the style of bowling became legal just two years later.

Lillywhite, of course, is another famous name in the annals of cricket history with all three brothers John, Fred and James, playing first class cricket. John was also an astute businessman and opened his sports store near Piccadilly in 1863, selling high class sporting equipment servicing, as well as cricket and football, sports such as Polo and Croquet.

The store remained in the locality under the same name until it was bought in 2006 by a gentleman named Mike Ashley who somewhat changed the image and the name to 'Sports Direct'!

Teddy's last match for Middlesex was against Nottinghamshire in Nottingham in 1877 when he was aged 40.

He subsequently played a few games for Minor County, Bedfordshire.

Towards the end of his life, in 1900 Teddy was interviewed by A.W. Pullin researching for his book 'Talks with Old Cricketers' and he was given a whole chapter to himself.

Whilst discussing his career he broke off to say, with typical modesty 'But I really do not care to continue talking about my own performances. There is nothing in them that I think is worth enlarging upon'.

He was wrong!

He became a director of Taylor Walker, the family business, was a Justice of the Peace and was appointed Deputy Lieutenant of the County of Middlesex, a very important dignitary at the time.

In later life he continued to take a great interest in the game and watched his share of cricket, although he considered that modern players were more interested in averages than his generation had been. He referred to this as 'average hunting'.

In 1900 he was interviewed for a journal and said 'It is an age since I played cricket but I love it yet'.

Teddy in later years, pictured outside the family house with his beloved dog 'Spot'.

He died just after Christmas, having entertaining many family and friends at Arnos Grove over the festive period, and had been attending to business matters almost up to his death.

He was a very popular man and was highly regarded by all, the people of Southgate in particular, as he strolled around the village with his much loved dog, 'Spot'.

The value of Teddy's estate, £1,598,177, was a remarkable amount of money at the time, worth in excess of almost £30 million today! Benevolent to the end he ensured all his sisters and their families were generously considered in his will, also numerous friends, and each member of his staff, now numbering over twenty.

Finally he bequeathed to various Hospitals, Societies, Churches and of course, The Cricketers Fund Society.

Russell Donnithorne Walker ('Russie')

Born: Arnos Grove 1842

Died: Regents Park, 1922 aged 80

First class career

Oxford University (1861-1865)

A Middlesex XI (1862)

MCC (1862-1878)

Middlesex CCC (1864-1877)

122 matches

3,840 runs

Highest score 104

142 wickets

Russie uniquely represented Oxford University for five consecutive seasons as a result of which a new rule was created whereby people could only play in four Varsity matches.

He was a right hand batsman and a round arm slow bowler and was very skilful in placing the ball through gaps in the field using a bat the handle of which was two inches longer than the normal. His favourite shot was when he dealt with bouncers and bumpers and struck them over his shoulder and high over the long stop fielder.

His batting style was regarded as unique, totally different to anyone else. At the beginning of an innings he often looked quite ordinary but as yet another carefully placed guide went quickly through the slip area it eventually dawned on people that these shots were not lucky, they were all deliberate.

He was a fine scholar and multi-talented and skilled in so many different areas, quiet, reserved and methodical.

Like his brothers Teddy and Donnie he played rackets to a very high standard (he, like brother Teddy 'held the racket' at Harrow) and at one stage he was regarded as the best amateur rackets player in the country. He was also a fine billiards player, a clever croquet player and more than competent at tennis.

He was a very keen fisherman and spent much of his leisure time fishing in the north of Scotland. He was a very keen bridge and whist player, a member of The Turf Club and an opera lover.

He became a barrister and initially had chambers in Lincoln's Inn.

Later in his life he became a Trustee of MCC.

A very well rounded individual, by all accounts.

The Times newspaper opined that he was 'probably the best all-round player of games who ever lived', a rather extravagant statement but there is no doubt of his extraordinary and varied talent.

The only sport he didn't like was golf and he was quoted as saying 'I only played once but if I ever went round a golf course again I should take a spade'.

Like his brothers he refused to wear protective clothing for most of his career but at the age of 32 in a match at Scarborough he received a mighty blow on his unprotected shin from the fastest bowler of the day, Tom Emmett.

Not out overnight he arrived on the following morning wearing pads and never batted without protection again.

Like brother Donnie he also travelled to play cricket abroad. He went to Paris with a combined MCC and I Zingari team in 1867 and in 1881 he played a match in Hong Kong alongside Lord Harris.

His last match for Middlesex was against Surrey at The Oval in 1877 at the age of 35 when although failing with the bat, he picked up 4 wickets.

Strangely, he was almost as well known for his rather unorthodox clothing as for his cricketing fame. In Edward

Rutter's book 'Cricket Memories' his sartorial appearance was described thus ' R.D. Walker's approach to the wicket with his well-known degage and his queer-shaped felt hat with a ribbon round it inspired one wag to say 'It looked more like a Punch and Judy show'.

Another scribe of the day described his appearance at Lord's with his brightly coloured Harlequin shirt and his 'pot hat'!

R. D. Walker.   F. Penn.   Lord Harris.   L. Hone.   F. A. Mackinnon.
A. P. Lucas. S. S. Schultz. Mrs. Hornby. Lady Harris. H. D. Maul. C. A. Absolom.
A. N. Hornby.   Miss Ingram.   V. Royle.   A. J. Webbe.

LORD HARRIS'S TEAM. Australia - 1879.

R.D. Russie Walker was a member of Lord Harris's MCC team to tour Australia in 1879 but only played a couple of matches.

There was an infamous incident at Sydney in the match against New South Wales when there was a full scale riot when a large section of the crowd, possibly fuelled by alcohol and certainly by gambling, were unhappy with umpiring decisions.

Lord Harris, never one to fight shy of controversy, wrote a long letter of complaint about the behaviour of the crowd. He sent the letter to his friend in England, V.E. Teddy Walker and asked him to ensure it was published in the Daily Telegraph.

This Teddy duly did and there was a considerable amount of correspondence from English people and Australians alike.

Russie moved out of the family house in Southgate and bought a Villa in Hanover Gate in Regents Park where he died in 1922, aged 80, the last survivor and the brother who lived longest. One of the many advantages of living in this beautiful London park was that Lord's was approximately 300 yards away!

Many years later his villa and others in the immediate vicinity were demolished to make way for the London Central Mosque, built and opened in 1977.

He gave away a considerable amount of the contents of Arnos Grove, sold other pieces at Christies and gave £1,000 to the 'Southgate Relief Committee'.

Throughout his life Russie had been an avid walker, always trying to walk at least two miles after breakfast and another two after lunch.

In his Regents Park days he spent many happy hours walking in the park with his 'Aberdeenshire' dogs and was known locally as 'the man with the dogs '. He maintained his fondness for billiards and invited many of the best players to his villa for challenge matches, which he invariably won. He also co-wrote a book on the game.

Naturally, he retained his interest in cricket to the end when he was not so mobile and was often seen at Lord's in his bath chair.

In the MCC Annual Report of 1923 the editor referred to 'The sad death of our old friend and colleague, R.D. Russie Walker, the last brother of the Walkers of Southgate, who have done so much for English cricket'.

His will was worth £348,439 and it included bequests to his butler, his cook, his coachman, his housemaid, and other miscellaneous staff.

Isaac Donnithorne Walker ('Donnie')

Born: Arnos Grove 1844

Died: Regents Park, 1898 aged 54

First Class Career
MCC (1862-1864)

A Middlesex XI (1862-1863)

Middlesex CCC (1864-1884)

294 matches

11,900 runs

Highest score 179

218 wickets

Brother Teddy maintained that Donnie was the best batsman of his day and his record would suggest that ignoring natural brotherly bias that assessment was probably close to the truth. Remarkably he played for Middlesex for 20 years and he succeeded Teddy as captain in 1873 captaining his county for 12 seasons.

He scored 102 on his County debut and famously, in 1865, at The Oval, he hit the ball out of the ground from the Surrey bowler, H.H. Stephenson.

He was a methodical, cultured and disciplined batsman who played mainly on the off side and was known 'to stand up fearlessly to the fastest of bowling '.

He was also a successful lob bowler as his record suggests, but he was not considered the equal of his elder brother, Teddy.

At school at Harrow he was regarded as having more ability than any of his peers but his performances at school were far less than his potential. Like most of his brothers he was a relatively late developer.

Strangely, for a group of cricketers who were so successful later in their cricketing careers the brothers were not at all successful when playing for their school in the annual Eton v Harrow match at Lord's where they only scored a total of 157 in 16 innings or at University where they managed just 170 runs in 23 innings.

Hardly a forerunner of things to come.

Each brother, in turn, would seem to start his batting career with a 'ducks egg' or two.

(Ducks, apparently, produce round eggs rather than oval ones, and this term was subsequently shortened to 'duck' (being out for nought!) this being the origin of the much used term.)

Donnie, in a Gents v Players match at Lord's on one occasion suffered the indignity of making two 'Ducks Eggs' in one match. This was, and is still known as 'a pair of spectacles', subsequently shortened to 'pair'.

This double failure was especially disappointing in this particular case as he had taken a £5 bet with Lord Harris that he would definitely score at least one run in his two innings. Only £5 lost on that occasion but on another occasion he rather rashly had a bet of £100 to £1 with a gentleman called Jack Dale that Cambridge would not win the 1872 Varsity match.

They did and he lost his £100.

These are the only two examples of his gambling prowess discovered. He either learnt a lesson or kept his winnings and/or losses private.

Two innings of Donnie's are regarded as his best.

In 1882 he scored 165 for the Gents against the Players and a year later, playing for Middlesex against Gloucestershire, he and Alfred Lyttleton added 341 for the 2nd wicket, with 226 of the runs coming in 100 minutes after lunch.

His favourite shot was the drive over cover point's head described by one pundit of the day thus 'He would pat the top of the ball with a flat horizontal bat, a marvellous stroke of his for the ball was off to the boundary as if it had been shot'.

It is believed that he learnt this particular shot playing indoor cricket at Harrow, against school rules, where, in the cloisters there was a window high up and if reached the shot would count for six runs. Practice made perfect in this case but sadly for his successors the practice was later disallowed by the Harrow staff.

Donnie too, was highly regarded as a fielder by his peers. Writing in Lillywhite magazine a journalist said that 'with Teddy bowling and with Donnie and Russie fielding at mid on and mid off respectively they were like two terriers watching a rat hole'.

Like all of his brothers he was a very competitive sportsman. Towards the end of his career in a periodical of the day he was described thus *'Mr I.D. Walker, a veteran of the cricket family, still shows perpetual youth in the cricket field, and makes good average scores for the Metropolitan County. As a mid off he has not his fellow'.*

Beautiful phraseology by the unknown writer.

The Walkers, in general, were not keen to wear protective clothing but Donnie initially started wearing just the one batting glove but, as bowling became faster he elected to wear pads and two gloves.

A classic example of the social gap at that time between 'gentlemen' and 'players' occurred in 1865 when Donnie was playing for Middlesex against Yorkshire at Islington.

He was batting against young Tom Emmett, one of the fastest bowlers around at the time and until recently a raw young coal miner from Yorkshire. Emmett bowled a ball which sounds as if it was very much like the 'wonder ball' bowled by Mitchell Starc to dismiss James Vince in the Perth Ashes Test of 2017. Effectively a fast left arm leg break with an enormous change of direction once it hit the pitch.

In identical fashion to Vince, Donnie was comprehensively bowled and again, in similar fashion Donnie stood his ground, completely nonplussed by the event, at which point the raw young bowler berated the Old Harrovian batsman with the immortal words ' Whar ar comes from they call that oot!.

No doubt Starc used similar words to those to Vince 147 years later.

In later life Tom effectively crossed the divide, so to speak, when he became cricket coach at Rugby School, a position he held for many years.

Donnie was the only one of the brothers, apparently, who took a genuine interest in statistics and averages and in his 19 year first class career he averaged 25.30, an extraordinarily high average at the time when the standard of pitches were generally so poor.

In fact, he kept very detailed records of his cricket and later when organizing Harrow Wanderers tours and other matches he produced extensive and comprehensive reports on the season which he distributed to team members.

In 1878/9 he was selected to captain MCC in Australia but unfortunately he was unable to go due to the illness of his brother, Arthur.

A measure surely, of the closeness of all the brothers.

Sadly Arthur passed away before the end of that year.

Donnie travelled extensively in the off-season and travelled to Japan, China, Hong Kong and San Francisco amongst many other places.

In 1877 he arranged a game against Bombay Gymkhana …… away!

In fact, he was in India on business and together with a few friends and some local cricketers he was able to raise a side to play against the Parsees of the Bombay Gymkhana Club. His team, entitled Mr I.D Walker's XI, won by 21 runs and the home players were much impressed by Donnie's batting and his running between the wickets. The home captain stated that 'there was much for the Parsees to learn from the play of Mr Walker'.

Strangely enough, some nine years later Donnie was a member of the MCC team which played against the first Indian team to tour the UK, The Parsees, and he and W.G. Grace added over 100 for the first wicket. The Parsees were not especially strong and MCC won the match easily by an innings, with Donnie (5-29) and W.G. with 7-18 and 4-28, instrumental in their defeat.

In 1895/6 Donnie and two friends travelled on the Orient Liner to Australia and needless to say they were able to play three games of cricket in Sydney and Melbourne.

Even whilst abroad he never lost his interest in or dedication to Middlesex or Southgate cricket. His letters home would always include important and relevant comments on both.

Soon after his retirement as captain of Middlesex he was presented with a cup at Lord's with virtually every County player of his time subscribing. In response he made a very moving, heartfelt and articulate speech of gratitude thanking his cricketing comrades for their friendship throughout his career.

He was a quiet man and not comfortable in public speaking but spoke from the heart on a very moving occasion.

Many believed he could have continued to play County cricket for another couple of years and to prove that point he actually scored 50 and 27 in his final match for Middlesex.

After he retired from County cricket he devoted much of his time coaching boys at Harrow School and spent virtually every day of the summer at his old school. He was very highly regarded by all there and many considered he was the best cricket coach the school had ever had.

Donnie, it seems was not a forceful type of teacher and his coaching methods were in no way boisterous or too overpowering.

His advice to Harrow boys was simple 'When bowling keep the ball straight. When batting, hold the bat still and straight and do nothing at all with it on a difficult wicket. Wait until a really bad ball comes along'

Simple but sensitive and effective advice.

A group of Old Harrovians had played a few club matches before but In 1870 Donnie was asked by P.M. Thornton, a contemporary of his at Harrow, who played a few games for Middlesex, to really put the team on the map officially. Donnie became very active in the Club's development, organizing tours to the North of England and increasing their fixture list. These tours were over two weeks and to such places as Darlington, Leeds, Liverpool, Middlesbrough and York. Donnie organized the annual tour, arranged the fixtures and invited the players.

This continued until his death after which his great friend, A.J. Webbe, took over the duties.

After the Great War, in 1918 the constitution of the Harrow Wanderers Club changed, the fixture list increased and all old boys of the school became eligible to play.

Lord Hawke, an Old Etonian, a fine cricketer and later an instrumental figure in cricket administration but not a great lover of all matters Harrovian, made the comment, in an entirely respectful manner that Donnie Walker was more Harrow than any other Harrovian he knew.

Donnie would have been extremely proud of such a comment.

He was so highly admired by Harrovians of all ages that a tablet was placed in the school chapel in his memory.

The inscription was:

To the memory of Isaac Donnithorne Walker this tablet is dedicated.

Loyal, wise, patient, in quiet friendship and in summer games he gave to the boys of Harrow sound teaching in manly play and the example of an upright life: serving the school as one who recognized in all effort a higher service still.

In how many things he ministered thou knowest very well.

A fine tribute to a fine man.

He died quite suddenly in 1898 after a short illness, aged just 54. The County match between Middlesex and Kent was postponed so that players of both teams could attend his funeral and two days after his death in 1898 flags were flown at half mast in his honour during the Eton v Harrow match at Lord's.

A highly respected cricketer and gentleman.

Christ Church and The Walkers

Christ Church as it was towards the end of the 19th Century.

The overall beauty of The Walker Ground is enhanced further by the magnificent Gothic Church nestling in its south east corner. The current building is the second to be built on the site.

The Weld Chapel was built in 1615, donated by Lord and Lady Weld who lived locally. The footprint of the original chapel remains in exactly the same position in the church grounds to this day. This area is used for the internment of ashes of people whose names are recorded in the Book of Remembrance. A lasting tribute to the original name is the splendid tennis courts opposite the church where the club is known as The Weld Tennis Club.

The foundations for the new Christ Church were laid in 1861 and finally consecrated one year later. The architect was Sir George Gilbert Scott who was a fine exponent of 19th Century Gothic Revival. The church was made of Kentish rag and Bath Stone and has a spire 180 feet high.

It is believed that the highly ornate windows are some of the finest collections of pre-Raphaelite stained glass in the whole of London. Amongst the artists who designed them was William Morris, still famous today for his fabric and curtain designs.

In fact, in the church there is a carved oak screen backed by a William Morris fabric.

The church and grounds were situated in part of the vast estate belonging to the Walker family and the building was mainly funded by the family.

The Walker family were, of course, originally Quakers but changed to Anglican which was regarded at the time as more socially acceptable.

There are various items in the church dedicated by or to members of the Walker family.

The 'Sedalia', the Latin word for seats, although in this case actually two seats and a shelf, were built in The Sanctuary to remember Vyell Teddy Walker.

In 1905 Teddy himself, gave instructions for a 'Lady Chapel' to be built in a given space near the north wall of the

Sanctuary and this was to be dedicated to his parents Isaac and Sophia and the Walker family in general.

Sadly he died in 1906 before the work was completed.

Christ Church has a peel of 10 bells rung every Sunday. The oldest bell was originally used in the Weld Chapel and was a gift of a Lady Joanne Brooke in 1616. It is now used as the Sanctus bell. All the other bells were donated by grateful parishioners.

The sound of church bells has truly aesthetic appeal in Southgate and in many Churches around the UK.

However, many a Southgate cricketer fielding at the bottom end on a Sunday evening may not necessarily have enjoyed the sound as much as others.

Strong ear-drums required!

The Reverend James Baird married Anna Maria Walker, one of the five sisters of the cricketing Walkers and was vicar from 1856 to 1893. He and his wife and family lived in the main house, Arnos Grove, and a private doorway was built in the east boundary wall to enable him direct access from the grounds of Arnos Grove. He was described as 'a good man' and there is a dedicated inscription in their memory on the west wall of the church.

All in all, the Walker family seemed to have a tremendous reputation for generosity not only with money but also of spirit and it would appear The Reverend Baird was of similar standing. He and his wife founded 'The Baird Memorial Homes' for the poor of Southgate in nearby Balaam's Lane.

He was a very popular man locally.

Anna Maria's aunt, Lydia Rawlinson Walker had married another vicar, The Reverend Thomas Sale, who had been incumbent at The Weld Chapel from 1829 to 1852.

So, from 1829 until 1893, 64 years with a short break between 1852 and 1856 each Vicar of this famous church had been married to a member of the legendary cricketing Walker family of Southgate.

All seven brothers and their parents were laid to rest in the large Burial Vault near the West door of the church. The Taylor family of Grovelands House with whom the Walkers had so many family and business connections were also buried in the same vault.

The Reverend Charles Peploe, who was another long-serving minister at the church, serving from 1909 to 1937, erected a screen across the chancel arch in memory of his wife.

Many years later a subsequent vicar, the Reverend Brian Mountford, had the screen removed as he considered it interfered with the architect's original design.

Brian played cricket for Southgate for a few years during his internship and was a useful batsman and wicket-keeper. He also represented London Diocese in The Church Times Cup Final in 1981 and he was very enthusiastic and competitive and wasn't always in agreement with umpiring decisions which had been given against him.

He is remembered fondly but those members who played with him would not be surprised that he was happy to go against tradition!

An ecclesiastical spin-off from the story of Christ Church is the fact that The Church Times Cup Final has been held at The Walker Ground every year since 1950.

The Reverend David Sheppard, of Sussex and England fame, represented Liverpool in the final in 1967.

One time counsellor to the England cricket team and Dorset Minor County player, Andrew Wingfield-Digby played for Oxford Diocese on a number of occasions. For a number of years he had been resident vicar at Christ Church, Cockfosters and played for the local club for a number of years.

Another very competitive cricketer.

This tournament is very competitive indeed with teams entering from as far afield as Leeds and Liverpool in the North and Canterbury and Bristol in the South. Most teams, certainly those who reach the final, contain a number of fine cricketers confirming the close connection between cricket and the church. There have been many keen and closely-fought encounters between the participants and some extraordinary performances over the years.

None more so than in 2017 when The Bishop of Shrewsbury, 56 year old Mark Rylands, scored a magnificent 86 for

Lichfield against London, who, unsurprisingly have won the competition more than any other Diocese.

In deference to its neighbour no cricket was played before noon at The Walker Ground on Sundays until as late as 1978 when the law was changed, much to the chagrin of The Lords Day Observance Society.

Since the game's infancy the relationship between cricket and the Sabbath had its ups and downs, to say the least. As far back as 1611 two men, a Mr Richard Latter and a Mr Bartholomew Wyatt, were prosecuted by the elders of Chichester Cathedral for playing cricket instead of going to church. They were found guilty and fined one shilling each.

Clearly, the people of that area had strong religious convictions because a few years later, in Boxgrove, a nearby village, six other men were also fined for playing cricket in a churchyard on a Sunday.

Whatever would they have thought about the all-inclusive Sundays of today's generation?

Together with its cherished neighbour, the beautiful Walker Ground, Christ Church sets the perfect seal on the area and helps to create a mellow atmosphere which brings memories of calm and happy days.

The Walker Ground Trust

In 1907 the last surviving brother R.D. Russie Walker, placed The Walker Ground in the hands of Trustees to be used for ever for the playing of cricket, football, hockey and any other games approved by The Trust or Trustees.

So it has proved, now incorporating squash and rackets courts, tennis courts and facilities for cricket, football, lacrosse and rugby football. Only hockey has fallen by the wayside with that sport's requirement for all weather surfaces but Southgate Hockey Club continues to thrive with their new home at Trent Park in Cockfosters and Russie would have been delighted with that, as he was not only President of Southgate CC but also President of Southgate Hockey Club.

The first three Trustees appointed by Russie were Mr John Bradshaw, nephew to the brothers as the son of their sister Emma Loveday and her husband, Royal Naval Captain, John Bradshaw, Mr Raymond Barker and Mr Eugene White. Eugene White became the forerunner of so many Club members over the years who were to devote so much of their spare time to the welfare of Southgate Cricket Club. Quite apart from being a Trustee he was secretary for 35 years and finally President for a further ten years until his death in 1932. The loyalty of his wife was surely proven by the fact that throughout that time she provided teas for all the players... totally free of charge.

The Trustees were given discretion to allow any other games they considered suitable to be played on the ground.

By giving the Trustees such latitude Russie showed considerable foresight as this enabled the Trust to manage the ground to take account of the changing needs of its users and to introduce new activities and the local cycling club was another example of Southgate residents taking advantage of the facilities bequeathed by the Walkers.

The role of the Trustees has increased enormously over the years and now with an annual turnover well in excess of £200,000. It is more of a small business than just a cricket club.

In the early days any one of the three Trustees could easily deal with the relatively small amount of administration except when there was a major capital expenditure such as the construction of the groundsman's cottage in 1923, when they and the rest of the committee at the time would work together in unison.

The Trust became a registered charity in 1950 and around that time Mervin Glennie, who was already Hon. secretary of the cricket club, became a Trustee, having retired early from his job as an executive with The Anglo Iranian Oil Company. Mervin, a former 1st XI batsman/wicketkeeper and a Cambridge graduate worked tirelessly for the Club for well over 30 years until his death. His garage was packed with cricket club and Trust paraphernalia, old photographs, deeds, minutes of meetings and many other items of memorabilia dating back to the very early days of Southgate Cricket Club.

He, in turn was very appreciative of former Trustees such as Sammy Saville and Rupert Burton for the work they had done for the Club in the years between the wars.

Subsequently, Martin Fletcher, secretary from 1961 to 1994 and Ricky Gunn who held a whole host of jobs at the Club, ranging from Colts Manager to Hon. Treasurer from 1970 onwards are perfect examples of people who have given so much of their time, totally unpaid, to the development of Southgate Cricket Club.

Mervin oversaw numerous projects over that time, including the completion of a third ground to the north east of the existing one, the building of an impressive new pavilion in 1967 and the introduction of squash courts at the same time.

However, by the time Mervin died in 1987 it was clear that the new seven day a week operation could not be managed on a totally voluntary basis and a salaried Admin Director was appointed in the form of Chris Sexton.

Chris, a member of both the cricket and the squash clubs was a constant presence at the ground, always available and always keen to further the reputation of The Walker Trust and each of its member clubs.

Middlesex County Cricket Club were especially thankful for his management of the ground in the period 1998 to 2011 when the County played numerous County matches, including full County Championship matches and 20 over matches.

The Trustees, in 1963 initiated an annual Fireworks Display at the ground each November when the ground is bedecked with various food stalls, children's entertainments and culminating in a show which attracts as many as 5,000 people from the Southgate area and beyond.

This is now regarded as one of the best of its type in North London and is an important part of the Trust's income each year.

The Walkers would have been extremely proud of how their Club has been managed over the 170 years or so of its existence and probably quite surprised how it has developed so positively since John Walker laid the original foundations.

Southgate Cricket Club...
The Legacy

John Walker founded Southgate Cricket Club in 1855, but, in fact it was initially called Southgate Albert, changed to Junior Southgate in 1870 and finally to Southgate in 1886.

In 1880 it was decided by the brothers and the existing committee members that the Club colours should be light blue, purple and black and the Club flag still flies proudly on the ground in those colours to this day.

163 years after John Walker founded the Club it goes from strength to strength and hopefully will do so for another 163 years at least.

The ground is still administered by The Trustees and the Walkers would probably be very surprised to learn that there are currently six full-time employees, two employed on the ground and four in catering and administration roles.

Towards the end of the nineteenth century the three remaining brothers Teddy, Russie and Donnie had less close connection to Southgate Cricket Club and in fact, Donnie and Russie moved to Regents Park, some 15 miles away.

The cricket club, however, continued to prosper and was a very popular place to play and watch cricket, as it is today.

One local resident, Tom Gregory, told the Palmers Green and Southgate Gazette that as a boy, towards the end of the 19th century he and his mates would bowl to the 'gentry' and if their bowling was successful they would receive a penny if they hit leg or off stump and their pockets were full but more often they were empty.'

Many years later, another local resident, a Mr N.B. Collyer, in 1951, completed the task of copying out in beautiful copperplate hand writing every Southgate match from 1855 to the present day. The work took Mr Collyer over 2,000 hours and the volumes have been retained and are still in absolute mint condition.

Early facilities on the ground would have been more or less non-existent as the players would just stroll over from the big house and return after the game for their evening entertainment.

Slowly, over time certain accoutrements were added as required:

1877: A 'changing tent' was bought from Colney Hatch CC at a cost of £10.00.

1890: The first pavilion of sorts is built but it became known as the 'tin shed' as it became cold, draughty and wet!

1909: The first permanent pavilion is built at accost of £340.00. The 'tin shed' is relegated to a storage area facility. To celebrate the occasion Russie Walker invited Harrow Wanderers to play against the home side. A foot in both camps so to speak.

1923: A groundsman's cottage is built in memory of R.D. Russie Walker who had died the previous year.

1929: An extension is built to the pavilion providing new washing facilities.

1952: At last, a bathroom is installed in the Groundsman's cottage!

1956: A second ground is completed in the North east corner of the main ground and can be accessed through a small avenue of trees. The new ground to be officially known as Chapel Field and the main ground as The Walker Ground.

1967: A most impressive new pavilion is built.

1994: A pavilion extension with new bar and lounge facilities is completed on the eve of a match between an England XI and the New Zealand Touring team in the first match of their tour of England.

Throughout the twentieth Century Southgate retained an impressive reputation through the standard of its play and the quality and beauty of its ground. Membership remained high throughout although there was a slight decline either side of the Second World War.

Nonetheless, the Club's reputation was high enough for them to be invited to play local rivals Hornsey at Lord's in two consecutive years, 1940 and 1941. In the second of these challenge matches Josh Tyler, many years later to be Club President, scored an extraordinary century before lunch.

Cyril (later Sir Cyril) Hawker played in both those special matches at Lord's.

Cyril Hawker, pictured above on the left of the front row and Josh Tyler, third from left in the back row.

The following message was printed on the official scorecard. *'In the event of an Air Raid good cover from shrapnel and splinters should be available under the concrete stands. Spectators are advised not to loiter in the streets after the game'.*

Good advice.

Cyril was captain of the Club throughout wartime and beyond from 1942 to 1951. He later became Chief Executive of The Bank of England, was appointed President of MCC in 1957 and Southgate in 1959. The 'Cyril Hawker' Trophy which he bequeathed to the Club to be awarded 'to a deserving member of the Club, on or off the field' is still awarded and is received with much pride by each recipient. The introduction of numerous other trophies and awards at the Club in recent years has meant that the citation has now been changed to 'The Player of the Year'.

Immediately after the war Southgate hosted Benefit matches for three of the County's favourite sons, Laurie Gray, Jim Sims and the one and only Denis Compton. The beneficiaries were delighted with the results and the generous responses from crowd attendances ranging from 6,000 to 9,000.

During the fifties the tiny old pavilion was a haven, surrounded by a host of roses, nurtured and cared for by the members seated behind a small picket fence. Woe betides any person, especially a small child, who would dare to enter the compound without invitation! On the other side of the ground, in the shade of the church, stood a small tea hut and queues at tea-time on Saturdays and Sundays snaked for some distance, sometimes including as many as 100 people enjoying their weekend game of club cricket and their afternoon cup of tea and slice of home-made cake.

So many top players represented Southgate during the twentieth century but arguably the three most notable cricketers produced by the Club during that time were Alan Fairbairn, Chris Payne and Phil Tufnell.

Alan, an Old Haileyburian, who scored a century on debut for Middlesex in 1950, followed by another in his second match, did not persevere with life in County cricket as he wished to pursue a legal career but his loyalty to Southgate Cricket Club remained undiminished. A fine left handed batsman he was captain of the Club from 1952 to 1958 and President from 1988 to 1990.

Chris Payne was on the County staff for two years, but despite scoring a near double century for the Second eleven, and playing a few County games, he retired from full-time cricket to become Southgate's most successful captain and many good judges considered him to be the Club's best ever batsman.

The highly successful Southgate team of the seventies pictured at Edgebaston in 1977 having won the National KO Cup.

BACK ROW: R. Ashby; M. Smethers; C. Payne (Captain); R. Musson; A. Wyatt; S. Young; N. Bishop; S. Rowe. FRONT ROW: R. Johns; P. Brown; R. Hailey; M. Dunn.

The team of all the talents of which he was an integral part for 10 years and captained from 1976 to 1979 was a multi talented group who won a host of trophies, including the

National Knockout Cup, the final of which was originally held at Lord's, but replayed and won at Edgbaston after the first game had been abandoned because of rain.

Finally, Phil Tufnell joined the Club in 1983 aged 15, and only played for 3 seasons but certainly left his mark as he took 95 league wickets at 16.48 each during his time with the Club. He went on to become one of England's best spinners and subsequently an entertaining TV personality.

The 21st century has brought mixed fortunes for Southgate Cricket Club as it has suffered four relegations from the Middlesex League Premier Division between 2004 and 2017 and so far, three promotions back.

One more to follow soon, hopefully.

Membership has however, always been strong partly due to a strong Colts set-up, and four teams, occasionally five, have played each Saturday of the season for the past 50 years or so although like most clubs around the UK, Sunday cricket, due to social and financial issues, has been severely restricted.

However, thanks to the foundations laid and standards set by the amazing Walker brothers of Southgate their Club continues to flourish.

So how would the Walkers compare their rather leisurely cricketing activities to the helter-skelter and frantic lifestyle of today?

There are memories of a match at Redbourn in Hertfordshire, for instance, where John Walker, his brothers and the rest of his team travelled leisurely in their horse drawn carriages with gentle refreshment stops at hostelries in Cockfosters, Potters Bar and St Albans on the way to the match.

Compare that to the chaos of joining the M25 on a Saturday lunch-time.

They would be impressed with the facilities on offer at professional and club level.

They would be sceptical of the use of such full protection, pads, box, gloves, thigh pads, chest protectors, helmets etc, as in general the brothers declined the use of those items which were on offer at the time.

They would have quite liked the coloured clothing used so much today as in much of their early cricket they would have worn similar outfits.

Russie, in particular, would have welcomed them.

They would enjoy T20 cricket as, they would accept that, it is basically the same game that they played; the same game as 4 day county cricket; the same as 5 day Test cricket;

Just a shorter version.

They would have loved the way that their two most loved venues, The Walker Ground and Lord's, have developed, but both retaining so many of the qualities and disciplines so prevalent in their day, yet moving forward as time moves on.

The Walker Ground, on a bright summer's day, as beautiful as any club ground in London. Lord's, the Mecca, steeped in history, retaining all its great traditions whilst adding modern but tasteful buildings all around.

So, on 27 March 1922 Russell Donnithorne Russie Walker died at his home in Regents Park, London and the direct link between an amazing cricketing dynasty and Southgate Cricket Club was over.

This blue plaque remains on display to this day at the former Walker family home in Southgate, Arnos Grove.

The Walkers at Southgate

John Walker
Played 127 games
Captain 1855-1864
President 1855-1872

Alfred Walker
Played 87 games

Frederic Walker
Played 79 games

Arthur Walker
Played 114 games

V.E. Teddy Walker
Played 175 games
Captain 1865-1869
President 1873-1905

I.D. Donnie Walker
Played 123 games
Captain 1870-1877

R.D. Russie Walker
Played 108 games
President 1906-1922

Made in the USA
Middletown, DE
11 April 2019